Principles of International Marketing Research

Principles of Export Guidebooks

Series Editor: Michael Z. Brooke

Principles of
International
Marketing Research

Len Groves

First published 1994

Reprinted 1999

Blackwell Publishers Ltd
108 Cowley Road
Oxford OX4 1JF, UK

Blackwell Publishers Inc
350 Main Street
Malden, Massachusetts 02148, USA

British Library Cataloguing in Publication Data
A CIP catalogue record for this book is available from the British Library

Library of Congress Cataloging– in–Publication Data
A CIP catalog record for this book is available from the Library of Congress

Typeset in 11 ½ pt on 13 ½ pt Garamond Light
by Aitch Em Wordservice, Aylesbury, Buckinghamshire, Great Britain

This book is printed on acid-free paper

Contents

List of Figures

Foreword

It is a pleasure to welcome this book on market selection and research, a most significant part of the export thrust, which is the subject of the sixth book in our series. Len Groves has acquired expert knowledge and is known for practical advice. His work is assured of a warm welcome from those puzzled by the complexities of the topic.

The Earl of Limerick, President,
The Institute of Export

Series Editor's Introduction

In launching the sixth book in this series of guidebooks to the profession of exporting, the series editor – along with others associated with the project – is pleased to welcome Len Groves as its author.

Like the book on trade and payments, *Principles of Export Marketing Research* is necessarily more technical than some in the series. The author's contribution to the development of you, the reader, rests on his long experience as a consultant in export marketing and I present this book with great pride to the exporting public.

All the books in this series are preoccupied with bringing products to foreign markets (what else is export about?) and this book – which reviews the subject of market choice – sets the scene at the start of the process from which all successful exporting stems.

May I welcome you, the reader, and hope to meet you again in the other books in the series which cover all aspects of export which you need to know – law (for the non-lawyer), transport and distribution, international marketing, international trade and payments, and export management in addition to the first book in the series which is a review of the whole subject.

The main focus of Len's book is on market research – how to investigate it and match the opportunities discovered.

Michael Z. Brooke

About The Institute of Export Examinations

The Institute is grateful for the initiative of Michael Z. Brooke, the series editor, and Blackwell Publishers in publishing this unique series of books specially written for the Professional Examinations.

The authors for the series have been carefully selected and have specialized knowledge of their subjects, all being established lecturers or examiners for the Professional Examinations.

The books have been written in a style that is of benefit not only to students of The Institute but also to commercial organizations seeking further information about specific aspects of international trade.

Professionalism in export is vital for every company if they are to compete successfully in world markets and this new series of books provides a sound basis of knowledge for all those seeking a professional qualification in export through The Institute of Export's Professional Examinations.

The book covers the following parts of The Institute's syllabus.

Export Markets: Selection and Research

Objectives of the Syllabus

To give students an understanding of the factors affecting the decisions involved in selecting export markets; the methods of market research and the setting up of an information system within the firm; in addition, to develop statistical skills of use in these and other activities.

Export market selection

1 How many markets?
  How this should be related to the firm's size, availability of qualified staff, resources and export experience.
  The dangers of fragmentation of effort.
  The need to concentrate on a limited number of key markets most likely to be profitable.

2 What influences market selection?
  Market potential (measured from the firm's point of view).
  The amount of adaptation required, that is similarity to home markets.
  Accessibility. Whether the markets selected can form a workable group.

3 Making the selection decision
  Collection of information on the factors listed above.
  Obtaining advice, e.g., BOTB, DTI, Banks and Chambers of Commerce.
  Visiting the markets.
  The concept of an international marketing strategy with markets selected for first and second stage development or expansion.

Market research

1 Why is market research needed?
The making of marketing and investment plans.
The development of products and the selection of markets in which they are to be sold.
The choosing of the appropriate marketing mix for each market.
Forecasting.

2 What sources are available?
Material available within the firm, e.g., sales analysis.
Published and unpublished statistical and other material.
Information collected by the firm's export staff, e.g.. on overseas sales trips, from overseas agents.
Information available from external computer bases.

3 What methods can be used to collect information?
Desk analysis – evaluating the sources and validity of information.
Analysis of statistical data.
Sampling techniques – random and quota sampling.
Design of questionnaires.
Interviewing – postal, telephone, face to face.
Observation.
Test marketing.

4 The code of market research
Differences between developed and undeveloped markets.
Decisions about work to be done by firm's own staff or to be commissioned from consultants, UK or locally based.
Factors entering into these decisions.
Evaluating the results of survey work.
Presenting results to management.
Cost/benefit analysis applied to market research.

5 The information system within the firm
The data provided by export market research can be regarded as part of this system which obtains information from a

number of sources, classifies it and analyses it, stores it and facilitates its retrieval by those who require it, preferably by use of electronic data processing.

Planning for international marketing

1 A sequence of decisions is taken by the firm planning sales abroad. After the decision to export, these are as follows:
 – Which markets to select
 – Then a plan for each market deciding:
 which channels of distribution
 policy on products, promotion, pricing and sales
 forwarding
 listing of export tasks
 allocation of tasks to staff
 day-to-day operational decisions
 – What investment to make in promoting sales internally.

2 Feedback on effectiveness of operations in each market leads to modification of these plans.

R.T. Ebers FIEx,
Director of Education & Training,
The Institute of Export

Preface

Target Readership

This book is broadly based upon the subject Export Markets, Selection and Research which is part of the syllabus for The Institute of Export Professional Examination Part 2 in Export Management. Thus, the primary readership will consist of those students who have successfully completed, or have been exempted from, The Part 1 examinations of The Institute. This body is based in London but another target readership will exist in members of other Institutes of Export or similar organizations situated in many other countries of the world. At the time of writing they can be found in Australia, Austria, Canada, Denmark, Eire, Finland, France, Germany, India, Israel, the Netherlands, New Zealand, Norway, Poland, Singapore, South Africa, Taiwan and the USA. These bodies are all linked by the International Association of Institutes of Export, the secretariat of which is based in the UK. The Association has held an annual conference in various member countries for 19 years up to 1992 and membership is steadily increasing.

A further target readership can be found in companies that are involved, or are intending to become involved, in the export of goods or services, particularly Export Sales and Marketing executives and administrators, while students of International Marketing will find this book of use and interest. This summary of potential readers is by no means exhaustive.

Objectives of the Book

Primarily this book focuses upon certain export activities as they really happen in the world of international business. At the end of most chapters there are questions which offer the basis for discussion and which are, in the main, questions that have appeared in the examination papers of The Institute of Export, London. In these questions the reader is presented with a problem or situation typical of those that occur in the world of exporting. The general approach of the book is to show that situations arise every day where a decision must be made. That decision may be defensive, such as buying time to investigate further, or aggressive; in the latter case, draw up your action plan and go for it.

As the potential readership of this book is so wide and the experience of readers likely to be diverse, there are certain to be many different reactions to the same problem or situation. This does not necessarily mean that some are right and some are wrong, just that they are different. The results of the various decisions may show some as more successful than others but if we had the benefit of hindsight we could all be millionaires.

One of the objectives of this book is to demonstrate safer ways of making decisions, based upon good quality, relevant and recent information. It is fine to fly by the seat of your pants if you keep winning but if you lose or keep losing you may be out of a job. The safer approach to decision-making requires a good records system, within your company, containing details of all aspects of past performance and with easy access to the system.

However, total reliance upon internal records would not be sensible. There is a big wide world out there, with a multitude of activities and interactions, many of which will not be relevant to your business, but plenty that will be. It is essential for you to know what they are and what is happening in all the relevant areas.

Good external sources of information include Government and trade statistics, business journals and serious newspapers, international fax directories and trade exhibitions, but usually the best and most current data is obtained by field research directed at customers, be they distributors or users. Field research may be conducted by your own staff, such as sales representatives on customer and market visits, by a professional market research organization or, best of all, by a combination of both.

Finally, this book examines techniques of planning – setting objectives which you consider to be achievable, given that the required resources to implement the plan are available. Such resources include finance, personnel and information.

1

Export Markets

There are more than 200 export markets if you look at the total of listed, and internationally recognized, countries. Some years ago, when there were fewer than this, an American company president said that there are 169 markets in the world and our aim is to sell to all of them. He was possibly speaking for Coca-Cola, McDonald's, General Motors or some other globally involved company.

Many companies do not have such ambitions but, if they do, they do not announce them publicly. Most companies do not have the required resources, or access to them, to contemplate such growth and will probably have no more than ten export markets.

The Nature of Export Markets

In the export field, you can deal with single markets, such as the United States of America, South Africa, Australia, China or Brazil, or with market groups such as the European Community (EC) or the Latin American Integration Association (ALADI). If you deal with the former there will always be differences of culture, language, regulations and so on, but even when you deal with the latter, differences will exist, such as interpretations of the rules, language and hidebound practices. The fact that countries are linked together for trade purposes does not mean that they are similar in all other characteristics; generally they are not.

Selling to export markets can be a difficult process, particularly if you have not done this before. Your domestic market seems safe and comfortable but to venture abroad ought to suggest that more care should be taken. In fact the same basic rules should apply. All customers, whether they are domestic or export, should be checked for financial status and credit worthiness. When you are contemplating entry into a new market, or expanding your export activity in existing markets, the scale of your operation is going to change.

Apart from considering markets from the territorial or geographical aspect, you must also look at markets by product, since most companies are selling more than one product. Your product range may consist of a number of closely related items or it may comprise several entirely different products or it may be composed of both of these elements. Often a company will have started its business with a single product or a closely-knit range of products and have later expanded its operation by diversification or acquisition, or both, to incorporate other products which may be linked to, or be completely separate from, the original product or product range.

For example, a company may have started out as a manufacturer of domestic heating systems, diversified into industrial and commercial applications and then acquired an ailing double glazing company, which brings into focus not only the maintaining of acceptable temperature levels, but also the reduction of noise levels. Later it may decide to venture into air-conditioning which will complement its other product fields.

It is not always possible to sell the whole of your product range to all of your buyers, even if they are broadly related, although you may be able to do so. Take the case of a company that markets five different products to eight separate markets; the statistics for the past year's trading are shown in figure 1.1.

Looking at these figures, you can see that sales to Market A, the home market, are about 25 per cent of the total sales which means that about 75 per cent are to the seven export markets. It is interesting to note that there is no territory where all five products are sold except the domestic market which could be due to any one or a combination of a number of factors, assuming that the product is launched first in the home market.

Figure 1.1: Analysis of sales by units of product and market during last year

Product Market	1	2	3	4	5	Totals
A	75	53	36	47	44	255
B	23	–	45	–	25	93
C	–	48	27	–	37	112
D	31	42	28	39	–	140
E	55	22	–	27	41	145
F	15	29	36	–	26	106
G	–	–	24	35	–	59
H	12	18	–	16	–	46
Totals	211	212	196	164	173	956

The factors include:

1 the length of time that the company has been trying to sell a particular product to a particular market;
2 the strength of the competition in various markets for various products;
3 the current objectives and resources of the company;
4 the demand for the product in a particular market;
5 the degree of adaptation of the product to meet the requirements of a particular market or markets.

You can probably think of many others.

If we consider the factors stated, the first would require details of previous years' performance which should be available but there are some strong performances in Market B for product three, in Market C for product two, in Market D for product two and four, in Market E for product one and five, in Market F for product three and in Market G for product four, so all markets have good sales, vis-à-vis the domestic market, in at least one product.

Factor 2 needs to be analysed in terms of how many competitors are present and whether they are indigenous to that market or are other exporting countries.

Factor 3 is based on a policy and resource allocation decision and improvements can usually be made.

Factors 4 and 5 are, to some extent, interlinked. The demand for particular products may have to be derived or it may depend upon a necessary degree of adaptation. The former will depend upon the persuasiveness of your sales forces and the latter will rely upon the availability of adequate resources.

Looking at market sales, markets C, D, E and F are strong and several combinations of any two of these would exceed the sales in the domestic market. The gaps, where no sales have been made to a market of a particular product, would seem to be an obvious target for expansion but, again, a reference to growth trends might suggest that existing sales of products within markets should be developed further.

The gaps in the grid are obvious targets for expansion of sales but this may be dependent upon the company's ability to come to terms with the requirements of factors 2, 3, 4 and 5.

It is important to recognize that there may be barriers to selling in certain countries. These may be official, arbitrary or commercial. Official barriers are generally down to protectionist measures to preserve particular industries and, at the present time, China is the victim of a number of punitive measures. To take an example, Spain and the south of France produce large numbers of beach shoes, or alpargatas, for the tourist trade. China can offer these shoes at a fraction of the cost of the European article and, therefore, punitive import duties were imposed on Chinese imports, which did temporarily stop the import of Chinese shoes into the European Community. However, the need to earn foreign currency simply meant that they exported the component parts, namely the soles and uppers, as separate products, the import of which was not penalized by Community regulations.

Arbitrary barriers are more difficult to deal with as they are usually based upon the relationship that exists between the two countries in which the seller and the potential buyer are situated. Competitiveness is not the only reason why business is developed, or not developed, between two countries; a more important one may be the political relationship that exists between the two nations, which is generally based on past events such as war, occupation, trade agreements and treaties.

The way to overcome this prejudice is to visit the particular market and find honest brokers or distributors who will be happy to represent your interests because they see a good living in it, but also because they do not subscribe to the official public view. Whenever there is a certain disharmony between nations, it is generally either the official or the majority stance. You can usually find one of the minority or neutral elements who can recognize a commercial opportunity, provided that there are no legal barriers.

Commercial barriers are also a headache to exporters. The exporter may be trying to sell to a market where the government of the country has a bilateral trade agreement with a country where your major competitor is based. In such cases, most favoured nation status may be linked to political manoeuvring and that is an extremely difficult combination to beat. One way to deal with this is to identify and contact the people who influence the business and offer them a sweetener.

One trader tells the story of a very large deal that he was negotiating to a particular market where the influential person had agreed the sweetener which was, of course incorporated into the price and the trader was informed that his company would most definitely be awarded the contract. Since his company stood to make £500,000 and he was on a 10 per cent commission, he was happily contemplating the diverse ways in which he could use £50,000 when he received the news that the influencer of the business had been jailed for corruption. The trader concerned ruefully told the story against himself to illustrate the fact that no deal is certain until the contract has been signed and, even then, no profit can be certain until payment has been made.

There are many markets where the person or persons who make the final decision about which company gains a contract will expect or, in fact, require that a part of the price agreed is reserved for their account. Companies must be aware that such practices are common and decide whether or not they want to be part of such a scenario.

It is not correct, however, to suggest that all export deals are conducted along these lines. Most of the day-to-day small to medium-sized contracts do not include this dimension nor do many larger ones and most companies take a pride in the fact that they conduct their business in a proper manner. The problem that exporters face with open or straight forward deals is that the profit margins are slim. There is little room for slippage in your costings, and a sound little contract can easily become a loss-maker.

It is extremely important that exporters understand the risks that are involved and how these can be reduced by handling the business in a specific way. If, for example, you are trading in a commodity such as the product of an annual crop, you may see your most rewarding course as taking a position, that is you either trade long or you trade short. A long position is one where you buy but do not sell at the same time because you expect the market price to rise so that you can sell later at an enhanced profit. The main dangers of taking a long position are that, if the price rises excessively, your sellers may default but if you (and possibly your competitors) have misjudged the size of the crop, you may find that there are more sellers than buyers and the price will fall and you will end up in a loss-making situation.

A short position is one where you sell but do not buy at the same time. In basically depressed market conditions, securing sales may be the major task. There will be plenty of sellers and relatively few buyers, so that every sale that you make reduces the overall residual demand. If the selling origins depend heavily upon their sales of a particular crop for a significant chunk of their foreign exchange earnings and, if the crop proves to be average or better, the short seller should be on a winner but if the crop fails in a major producing country, prices will rocket and the short position could result in disaster.

That is the scene if you are trading commodities but, if you are a manufacture, your approach will be different. You want a full order book stretching away six months, nine months, a year or more into the future so that you can produce as near as possible to your full capacity and you can work to the average cost concept. You will know, from past experience, that raw materials, components, power, labour and other costs are likely to fluctuate, although in some cases they are more likely to rise than fall and you can calculate your prices accordingly. Sometimes your prices will be competitive and sometimes they will not but a regular evaluation of the market situation should enable you to even out the variances.

How Many Markets to Choose?

This really means how much business can you handle and the following criteria should be used to reach that decision.

1 The size of your operation.
2 The resources that are available or potentially available.
3 Your experience in the export field.

If you are a small company with sales, say, of between £500,000 and £1m and with profit margins of 10 per cent, your chances of making significant progress in the export field are relatively slim but certainly not impossible. You must remember that, just as there are small, medium and large companies in your country, the same range of company size exists in other countries and you may be able to build up relationships with some of these.

Obviously, if you are planning to expand, your resources must be capable of dealing with this expansion. Resources are mainly financial which may mean bank borrowing or share calls but, in the longer term, will also mean qualified staff and adequate back-up facilities.

Newcomers to exporting are at a disadvantage, even if they have a revolutionary new product. The buyers may be suspicious of you or your product, or both, and maybe would prefer to deal with a company based in their own country.

Let us explore the implications of these criteria. If we ignore the statement made at the beginning of this chapter, the answer to the question 'how many markets?' is theoretically and practically simple. You take on as many markets as you can realistically handle. You can always add to them if things go well.

Sales representatives are in a dilemma. They have submitted targets of what they feel can be achieved and they have been rejected. They are presented with targets which, if achieved, will enable management to reach their overall objectives. If the representatives do not accept these new targets, they can be dismissed. If they do accept them and fail to reach them, they can still be dismissed.

It is incumbent upon managers to ensure that they have a firm grasp of what is a viable target in a particular market and have regular planning and sales review meetings with their sales representatives.

The basic theory of sales forecasting is straight forward, but the practical implementation is certainly not. The theory is based upon last year's sales less lost accounts due to insolvencies, takeovers and other factors, plus anticipated new business.

In practice the last year's sales' factor is undeniable; it has happened and, although in the case of a takeover, you may be able to get back some business, it is unlikely to happen quickly as your competitors may already be dealing with the new owner.

The problem areas lie in the other factors; repeat purchase cycles are at least credible and the representatives hope that they can achieve them. Anticipated new business incorporates sales of new products to existing customers or market territories, sales of existing products to new customers or markets and sales of new products to new customers or new markets.

The sales representatives will generally tend to relate the amount of time spent and the degree of encouragement or non-rejection received, when trying to sell a new product or when selling to a new customer or market, to their perception of future success, and this will tend towards an optimistic forecast of these activities.

A company may be embarrassed by any significant under- or over-achievement by a representative or the sales force as a whole unless they monitor the situation carefully so that they know what is actually happening and can take appropriate action.

In many companies today this means relying on periodic, say weekly, computer printouts showing how much business has been done during the period, analysed by product, market and representatives. The purpose of setting up such a system is to enable management to monitor performance against targets, taking into account seasonal variations. Unless you are selling fast-moving consumer goods where the repeat purchase cycle is as high as weekly, you should not be concerned with shortfalls or excesses if the average remains steady. If you are selling consumer durables, your repeat purchase cycle will spread across several years and downward or upward trends will take longer to detect. If you are selling capital goods, your targets must be viewed from a longer-term perspective. For example, a sales representative for computer systems may have been set a target of sales of one system at a value of £500,000 per year. In 1991 no sales may have been achieved although a great deal of time has been spent with one prospective client. In 1992, two systems are sold, one to the aforesaid 1991 customer and one to a new customer, so that in terms of achieving the allocated sales forecast, in 1991 it was zero per cent and in 1992 it was 200 per cent.

It is obviously difficult to enter a new market. The buyers may not know your company and they may not know your product or, if they do, they will have no experience of it. Your product may be well accepted in your existing markets but you must be prepared to adapt it to meet the needs of a new market.

It does not help you to sell if the product requirements of the new market are different, even if you have sold to a number of export markets. If you do not, or cannot, adapt the new market will not buy, and this may be a requirement demanded by law; if you do not adapt, you do not sell.

If you are planning to attack a new market territory, new in the sense that you have sold none of your products there before, apart from the desk research that you may do and any field research that you may commission, a market visit is essential. This should be carefully planned and, ideally, should consist of a team, drawn from different parts of your organization such as sales, marketing, finance and export administration. Every member of the team should have a specific brief and should be encouraged to write up findings relating not only to the terms of the brief but also to any other matter that is considered relevant to the member's area of activity. If yours is a small company you may not be able to spare four persons for a period of two weeks but companies must make their arrangements according to their resources. The market visit will be covered in depth in a later chapter.

Questions for Discussion

1 After two years of exporting part of their product range to Belgium and Holland, CBC Electronics Ltd now wish to expand their export activities as follows.
   (a) Selling more of their product range into the same market.
   (b) Exporting to new markets.
   As Export Marketing Director, what factors would you take into account when planning to meet these objectives?
2 A market can be a part of the world, a specific product or a type of product. Explain what is meant by this statement.

2

What Influences Market Selection?

This chapter is designed to reinforce and develop key areas and to examine new concepts on a topic partly considered in the previous chapter. The four criteria that will determine the selection of new markets are:

1 market potential;
2 the degree of product adaptation required;
3 accessibility of markets; and
4 the dangers of fragmentation of effort.

Market Potential

Acceptable levels of estimated sales and profitability will differ from company to company, according to individual circumstances and objectives. Some companies may be seeking an outlet for an over-capacity of production and may be prepared to accept the principles of marginal costing in their calculations of target profits. Others may be looking for markets that are viably free-standing. In either case it is essential to establish that sales to any market do not reduce the overall profitability in anything but the short term. When you are contemplating entry into new markets, be it by territory or product, the main criteria must be the present level of demand for the product, the recent growth trend and your estimate of the future growth. In other words, you need to be able to determine, as accurately as possible, how much business you can expect to do and how much profit you think you can make.

In some companies, sales representatives are required to set a target of sales and profits for the coming year. In others, they will be set a target by the company.

If these targets are broadly achieved, they will be reasonably satisfied, assuming that the company has accepted the forecasts. The sales representatives have compiled these forecasts upon a basis of projected sales to existing customers where a pattern of business has been established and the hope of breaking into new markets on the strength of past experience. It is important that the company should understand the reasons for and motives behind such forecasts and offer back-up where necessary.

A progressive company with a dynamic outlook should recognize where a viable opportunity exists and make every effort to exploit it to the full.

Sales representatives are at the sharp end of the marketing scene and the good ones will know their product and their markets. They will also know the competition and what is preventing them selling in certain territories.

The company should encourage its representatives to confide their problems and should provide them with back-up. Most of them are thrusting extroverts who will thrive if they get support and will become discontented if they do not.

You will find a variety of competitors in most markets. There are the big companies who use their size and financial muscle to hurt the smaller competitors by offering goods for a period of time at a loss-making level to burn off the competition; you must be aware of this scenario. There are also big companies who take a paternalistic view and are basically saying that they can give buyers the goods and the service they require so why buy from others?

In one respect, at least, they are right – if there is a serious problem. Let us suppose a shipment of goods worth £100,000 is made and the goods are faulty. The buyer rejects the goods and if, after an independent survey, the goods prove to be faulty, the big supplier can afford to take the goods back and replace them. For the small supplier this could pose a serious problem that the supplier will find difficult to handle.

Most of the competitors in a market, in purely numerical terms, are likely to be small to medium sized companies who are generally looking for a fairly modest and basically safe sector for their business and many of these may be scared off by the degree of competitiveness that they find in the market.

For a small company this may be a sensible decision because it probably means that it has looked at the market potential, has identified aspects that it does not believe it can handle and backed off. Timing is always important in such decisions and, looking back, after the decision has been taken, the small company may see that, if it had hung in there, there could have been rich pickings, but it is important to realise that, if things had gone wrong, the small company could have been wiped out.

The assessment of market potential is, after all, an arbitrary decision. You are using your judgment to determine how you think you can perform in that market now, and in years to come. You should always take the gamble to proceed if the odds of succeeding are at least 60/40 in your favour.

The Degree of Adaptation Required

The amount of product adaptation required is a very sensitive subject. Ideally a company wants to market its products to new markets with no adaptation but this is rarely possible. Every market, however, has its own special properties and some adaptation will be necessary. These changes could include the following:

1 product: sizes, colours, safety features, packaging;
2 promotion: available media, possibility of in-store promotion;
3 price: foreign currency pricing, competitive edge; and
4 place: channels of distribution.

Generally, the degree of product adaptation should not be a problem. Most exporting companies can adjust to buyers' requirements in respect of size, colour and packaging of their product. Safety factors need more work but should not be impossible. Media advertising and in-store promotion are usually a matter of finding out what the scenario is in the new market and following suit. As regards price, your company should never be afraid of pricing your products in the currency of your customer. Foreign exchange cover is readily available and, if your bankers cannot handle this, set up an arrangement with a branch of your bank that can. It is vital that you establish sound channels of distribution for your products and this will involve a lot of work. You must visit the market and you must understand its method and philosophy. A good distributor is someone who understands and accepts your objectives and who demonstrates that he can support you adequately. Apart from using the market visit to familiarize yourself with the market conditions and possibly to set up an arrangement with a local distributor, you can also study the ways in which existing sellers are operating. Never be too proud to copy a successful marketing approach. A useful way of determining how much adaptation will be required is to send samples of your product to prospective buyers and to ask them if the samples meet their requirements. If the answer is in the affirmative, you are then left to negotiate such matters as price, delivery and payment terms. If the sample needs some refinement, the prospective buyer will presumably tell you why it is presently not acceptable and you will have the opportunity of examining the feasibility and cost of the required adaptations.

Obviously some products do not lend themselves to the sampling method because they are expensive to produce and send to your prospective new buyer. In this situation you need to obtain in advance a precise specification of the buyer's requirements and determine whether or not you can provide this and at what cost.

In an extreme case you could find that, by following all the requirements of the buyer, you would be making virtually a new product, possibly because the technology of your product is not as advanced as that of competitors already selling to the new target market, and if you wish to persist in your efforts to sell there your only chance is to go back to the drawing board.

Another idea might be to consider allowing a local manufacturer to produce under licence and pay royalties. This would mean that the product would be made in accordance with local requirements and, although the return might be lower than you would normally find acceptable, after the initial period of setting up the project, your own resources would not be used. An alternative to this would be to establish a joint venture with a local manufacturer, where you supplied components and your partner put them together in a manner that would satisfy the local market.

Accessibility of Markets

Accessibility of the new market is a key to the ease of operation. If it is adjacent to one of your existing markets, you will probably find that you have less difficulty in interesting and reaching buyers in the new territory.

Selling to one or more countries in a market group, such as the European Community, is in theory easier than selling to individual countries. One tends to think that the market group members will have basically the same requirements while individual markets will have different needs and involve different considerations.

In practice, if you look at the spread of the members of the European Community, you will have a wide disparity of costings between shipping to, say, Eire, Northern European members, the United Kingdom, Italy, Spain and Portugal and this may depend not only upon the regularity of opportunity to ship from your homebase to these territories but also upon the cost of so doing. This latter consideration will partly depend upon the volume of traffic between your country and the particular market and may also partly depend upon the nature of the service available, for example container or break-bulk. Containerization has great advantages such as security and possibly lower marine insurance premiums but only if you can sell full container loads. Shipping part container loads with another cargo may be more expensive to insure because the container must be unstuffed at the port of discharge whereas, on full container load terms, the container can be unstuffed at your buyer's premises.

Where you are already selling to, say, Belgium, it should be possible to use the existing market as a launch pad to neighbouring countries such as Holland, Luxembourg, Germany and France. Certain aspects of the marketing mix such as advertising and technical literature, will need little or no adaptation because these will be presented in the two languages of Belgium, namely French and Flemish. French is spoken in Luxembourg and, of course, France while Flemish is very akin to Dutch. You will find that, particularly with technical literature, it is already being produced in a number of languages by your competitors and you must do the same.

Having said that, you should not automatically reject accessible single or group markets because their requirements are fundamentally different from those of your existing markets. Accessibility does not simply mean that the potential market is proximate to an existing market or your own country but will also embrace other markets that although more distant in terms of mileage, may offer good potential demand for your products while at the same time having good, if somewhat lengthy, voyage access by ship.

It is a golden rule in business, or it should be, that you have not secured your profit on a deal until you have received payment in full. If you are giving a buyer payment terms of any kind that allow possession or title to the goods before paying, you are at risk. Therefore, the creditworthiness of your buyer must be ascertained and found acceptable. Also, if you relate your assessment of risk to the rating given by a credit insurer, such a NCM, the country itself may be penal-rated because of economic or political problems in that country and you must include the additional premium in your costings.

This is a vital area to consider when deciding which markets to select. The adrenalin of the eager salesman must be measured against the risk of not being paid. Export markets are basically unknown territory, or at least foreign territory. You may be very familiar with a market where you have sold for many years and when you have the opportunity to sell to a new buyer in that market, your guard may be down, because you have had few problems in the past. There are cowboys operating in every market and while there will be some in markets that you have not entered, there will also be some in your existing markets. Market expansion carries a latent credit risk and nothing should ever be taken for granted.

Accessibility does involve ease of reaching and servicing a market; it also involves being comfortable with the conditions prevailing in that market. Probably the most important of these will include creditworthiness and financial status of the buyer. Always check out these areas with a reputable credit reference company. If the buyer wants open credit, whatever his status, having credit insurance is advisable.

Dangers of Fragmentation of Efforts

Where a company is seeking to expand significantly into export markets and the salesforce is motivated to push back the frontiers, there is a grave danger that these efforts will be fragmented. Even if your company has adequate resources to attack several markets at the same time, it is wise to proceed with some caution. Every new market needs careful planning, management and monitoring and unforeseen problems can arise which require head-to-head attention. Most companies have one or two proven troubleshooters but few have four or five and it is virtually impossible for one such problem-solver to handle more than one situation at the same time.

There are, however, a number of situations where exporters may be tempted to venture into several markets simultaneously. These include:

1 the markets are similar to each other or the existing markets where the company is operating;

2 the company has a range of products and believes that these have different potential profitability in different markets and therefore constitute separate market operations;

3 the product or products may be at an advanced stage of development that is ahead of the competition and the company wishes to maximize its advantages.

All of these situations are understandable and most companies would certainly consider a multi-new-market operation but they should also look at the possible dangers which include:

1 overstretching of resources so that some, or possibly none, of the new markets receive adequate support to establish and develop the sales in each market;

2 monitoring a multi-faceted activity is difficult and management may look at the overall performance rather than individual products in the various markets, so that the overall position may conceal specific problems in some area.

Developing these points further, let us consider similarity of markets. Earlier in this chapter we looked at degrees of adaptation required and proximity to existing markets. If your company is studying, say, five new marketing territories and they all score favourably in respect of low adaptation and close proximity, you would be very tempted to go for all five. Resources might be adequate to do this but you must investigate to what extent plans for expansion in existing markets would be affected. Looking at the budget available for, say, the next year's forecast business, provision should have been made for any projected growth in existing markets and, where applicable, entry into new markets. If the total forecast sales fit into the budget available, there should not be a problem. However, in practice this is rarely the case and different managements may take different views. One approach could be to view growth in existing markets as more reliable because the company is established there, which in a battle for a slice of the budget cake could seriously affect attempts to enter new markets and cause the salesforce concerned to become frustrated and disheartened. Another view might be to say that the company needs should be given priority, since the company can always develop existing markets later. To a sales representative who has established good records of gradually expanding sales to existing markets this could be like a slap in the face and, perhaps, cause them to feel discouraged and less committed to expansion.

The effect of management decisions of this kind will only be seen after the decision on priorities has been taken. There are usually alternative courses of action, one of which will be preferred for relative profitability, continuity of business, overall growth, market share, market dominance and other reasons.

The facility to monitor performance against targets will largely depend upon how the management structure is arranged. Where you have a number of products and a number of market territories, you probably need an export manager who will co-ordinate sales efforts to all market territories but in management you must not make the span of control too wide for one person to handle. For example, if your company is exporting ten products to eight countries, you would, in theory, have ten export product managers, each of whom would have two assistant managers covering four markets. This is only an example, since the responsibilities are likely to be regionalized on a proximity basis. Your eight territorial markets might be Belgium, Holland, France, United States of America, Canada, Iran, Turkey and Pakistan. In this case you would probably have three assistant product managers for a particular product for:

1 Belgium, Holland and France;
2 USA and Canada;
3 Iran, Turkey and Pakistan.

In some cases, where some products are closely related, one export product manager could take responsibility for several products and the assistant product managers would similarly be responsible for that group of products in their territory.

Considering the situation where, because of potentially different profitability, markets may be regarded as separate entities, this is a tricky area. The fragmentation of the markets may prove beyond management to supervise and control. To take the earlier example of eight new markets covering ten products, you could be looking at eighty separate markets plus those you already have which, for most companies, could not be handled in terms of personnel. You must look at projected sales and profits and come to a decision about what personnel you can afford to service and manage these markets.

If you are on a roll and your products are setting the trend in one or more markets, you may decide to invest heavily in all resources, including personnel, in order to achieve your goals. The wisdom of such decisions will only be verified later.

Questions for Discussion

1   Burgess Meredith Plc manufacture and market surgical instruments and hospital operating equipment to the United Kingdom and other European Community markets. The sales within the European Community have shown a steady growth of about six per cent a year over the past five years. Research into other market territories has indicated potential sales to Brazil of about £10 million per annum but, if these indications were realized, your limited production capacity would restrict the continued growth to European Community markets where currently sales are running at £75 million a year. Your company, IMC Ltd, has been retained as market development consultants.

Prepare a report to your clients with your recommendations on how to proceed.

2   Acorn Tractors Ltd has been manufacturing and marketing tractors and agricultural machinery and equipment since 1975. Five years ago, they entered the export market and during that period built up a sound business in Italy and the Netherlands.

The company is now considering an expansion of its export business to other European Community countries but is also looking seriously at the potential of Eastern European countries following the recent political changes.

It has engaged your company, Export Consultants Ltd, to advise on how to proceed. What are your recommendations?

3

Making the Selection Decision

This is the most important stage in the export process so far considered for it is at this point of the pre-planning that you are going to commit your company to a course of action. In the previous chapters we have studied the different types of market by product and by territory and by product within territory. We have compared the opportunities that exist and even some that may be created and we have examined the dangers of attempting to spread resources and efforts too widely. By inference we will also have thought about concentrating these too narrowly. Now we have to be certain that we are ready to take the decisive step that will set us on the road to successful export expansion.

It is desirable to produce a guaranteed blueprint for success and, although there are very few circumstances in which success is certain, three activities – if properly executed – will give us a good chance of achieving a satisfactory performance. These are:

1 collecting information and seeking advice;
2 visiting the markets; and
3 drawing up an international marketing strategy.

Collecting Information and Seeking Advice

The availability of adequate resources is vital to any business enterprise and, of course, insufficient funding will generally preclude the possibility of expansion of your commercial activities. Money, however, is only significant if it is used to advantage. This involves investment in product, people and information; in some respects, the obtaining of good information is at least as important as any other element. Information is judged in this context by its relevance, recency and accessibility; in some countries the quantity and quality of available marketing data is very impressive, in others, it is not.

The first source of valuable information should be from your own company's records. These are certainly relevant and accessible and should be maintained to a standard that makes them recent. Records are, however, by definition, reports of past events and planning is concerned with the future. We need, therefore, to be able to set past performance against the backdrop of the total scene in the markets where we are operating or are intending to operate.

Information from outside sources is therefore essential if we are to plan with understanding in the context of the complete market scenario. There are basically two types of information external to the company published and available statistics and the findings of field research.

A great deal of commercial information can be obtained in many countries from banks and government statistics at a modest cost. It must also be said that in many countries, the quantity of information is less than useful. A good back-up of data is available from market research companies who are able to provide details of general findings in a market, often referred to as omnibus research while, of course, you can commission a market research organization to carry out specific research into your own particular fields of interest.

You can also conduct your own field research and this course of action is often preferred by companies who are involved in the marketing of industrial products where the number of buyers is considerably fewer than in consumer or consumer-durable marketing.

Visiting Markets

Many companies do, in fact, conduct their own field research through their sales force on market visits. The industrial survey is probably better carried out by sales representatives rather than by a market research company. This is because the representatives know their products thoroughly, have a good relationship with their customers, have a good knowledge of the business that they have done, or want to do, and can think on their feet. The market visit, in this context, can be invaluable, because the representatives can renew acquaintances with old friends or can meet clients for the first time. There is nothing better than meeting the people who have the buying influence to set up a good, enduring relationship.

A market visit must be carefully planned and executed. You must have a clear idea of why you wish to visit customers, what you are seeking to achieve, or discover and how much time you need to spend with each customer. Are you intending to invite them to lunch or dinner, and have you told them? Apart from the individual visits to customers, you must allow yourself time to check out what is happening in the market. Sometimes buyers will tell you what is happening to them, but if they do not volunteer this information you should certainly try to find out as much as you can. Face-to-face conversation, if properly conducted, should yield more relevant and usable data than any other source, but careful pre-planning is essential to optimize the benefits of the visit.

It is not sensible to try to organize a market visit at very short notice except when the main purpose of the visit is to try to sort out a problem when the buyer will expect you to be there. Generally, however, where the decision to make a visit originates from your company rather than from an emergency, you have time to plan and a good way to handle this is for the sales manager or executive responsible for the particular market to ask the sales representative to write down a list of questions that will be asked, giving reasons, and for the manager to write down what he thinks should be asked. The manager should then have one or more sessions with the representative to determine degrees of priority for the various areas of questioning. It is very important that the manager handles this exercise tactfully since the representative usually has a superior knowledge of his or her market and customers and, sometimes, of the impact of the product in these areas while the manager will know, from his conversations with, and directives from, his superiors what will fit into the company's overall thinking.

It is important that the representative feels comfortable with the visit itinerary and plan as this will generally lead to an improved performance. If a representative is suggesting that six days are needed to complete a task while the manager is stipulating four or five days maximum, unless the representative has a record of over-long visits to markets, his or her requirement should be conceded. If the representative does have such a record, the manager must consider why the company is still employing this representative.

Market visits are a fact of life in exporting but there is no place for the casual approach. Basic details, such as flight times, hotel reservations and general expenses are usually part of company policy and the representative should establish before the visit takes place that what he or she is proposing to do is acceptable to the company. The itinerary should be planned with care, particularly if the representative plans to visit a number of towns or cities in the market territory. This is even more important if the market visit incorporates more than one market territory where these are adjacent or in the same part of the world. For example, if your company is selling to, or is contemplating selling to Australia, New Zealand and Malaysia and has no other markets or potential markets in Australasia or South East Asia, it makes good sense to incorporate all three territories into one visit, unless you have made a fairly recent visit to one or more of these countries.

The example quoted might require two or three weeks if you have eight customers to visit, say two in Malaysia at Kuala Lumpur, four in Australia with two in Sydney, one in Melbourne and one in Adelaide and two in New Zealand with one at

Christchurch and one in Auckland. For a start, if you are travelling from the United Kingdom or Northern Europe, you must
allow one day each way for travelling to the general region but
you must .recognize that while you may be able to see both
Malaysian clients in one day, it will take you at least another
day to reach Adelaide; on the following day you can visit your
Adelaide client and maybe catch your flight to Melbourne, where
you will probably have time to make your visit and catch the
plane to Sydney, possibly in time for dinner with one customer
there. After seeing the second Sydney client you take the plane
to Christchurch, where you visit your customer. Then a flight to
Auckland to see that customer which will probably be the day
after you arrive, and finally you board your flight home which
may be the next day or several days later, according to airline
schedules. If you are very lucky with flights leaving on time and
making the scheduled connections, and finding your contact
available when you arrive, with this sequence being repeated
throughout the whole trip, you can accomplish this visit in
eleven days, but do not bet on it. Always allow several days for
delays on long trips and never tell a customer in Australia that
you will be in his office at 9 am on Tuesday, 7th September if
you are setting out from the UK on 1st September – you may
even be a day out in your calculations if you are visiting another
market on the way.

Always come fully prepared for a visit. You need to know the
position of every contract that you have with the customer, the
state of any problems that you have, some idea of a solution
acceptable to your company and your ideas about repeat orders
and new business. It will help if you can appear relaxed with
the buyer and it is a good idea to open the meeting with some
personal chat – asking about the family, the golf handicap,
world events and politics and, in a session that is planned to
last for two or three hours including lunch or dinner, you can
certainly afford to spend twenty minutes to half an hour on the
preambles. The core of your discussions can then take place in
a friendly and relaxed atmosphere and you should have prepared a range of questions on all of the topics relevant to each
customer. It is essential that you find out the buyer's reactions
to your questions and whether he or she has anything to add

to what you have said. The face-to-face interview is a precious opportunity to glean useful information that could help to strengthen your relationship with the buyer and enable you to give an improved service and the opportunity should not be missed.

Where you are visiting a potential new market or a potential buyer in an existing market, relationships have to be built. It is best to present the profile of your company in clear terms, giving the buyer a copy of your company or group brochure and trying to achieve a reciprocal reaction. A relaxed approach is also recommended unless your company policy is to be aggressive and pushy. This is only advisable where you are confident that you can fulfil your promises; if you are not you may secure one contract which runs into serious problems later and no further business. Serious buyers who are new to you will have existing suppliers and, if you are making extravagant claims to be able to satisfy their requirements at highly competitive prices, they are bound to ask themselves several questions, such as: Who are these people? What do we know about them? Can we trust them?

When representatives return from market visits, they are generally required to write reports for management. These must include not only the topics that are discussed with the buyers but also a forecast of what business they think can be done in these territories; they will be expected to include these forecasts in their predictions for the coming months or years. While the format of the report should include all the guidelines agreed with the manager, it should also cover other matters believed to be relevant and potentially useful to market planning.

There are recommended ways of writing reports and all of them are arguably satisfactory. It is often useful to adopt the following structure:

1 location and duration of visit;
2 objectives of visit;
3 summary of findings;
4 detailed presentation about the various meetings;
5 conclusions;

6 recommendations and actions required; and
7 supporting data.

A market visit is a piece of field research and, as such, must be coherent and intelligible in the context of the objectives and reported facts. While the soft data aspect of the overall report is very significant because it reflects the attitudes of your buyers and the quality of your relationships with them, the hard data such as overall and individual demand, buying patterns, purchase cycles, size of normal purchase and your market share are vital for the confident development of future marketing plans.

In figure 3.1 we are looking at part of the report by a representative of a visit to Malaysia, Australia and New Zealand mentioned earlier in this chapter. It is good to set your sales forecast for the coming year against the background of past performance over, say, the last five years.

Figure 3.1: Analysis of unit sales and projected sales by buyer within market

Market Buyer	Year 1	Year 2	Year 3	Year 4	Year 5	Next Year
Malaysia						
Tan Soon	15	20	22	24	27	30
Heck Gu		10	12	12	14	20
Total	15	30	34	36	41	50
Australia						
Williams	124	209	273	395	404	425
Dennis	85	75	92	106	115	122
Sobell		14	25	38	46	54
Friend						30
Total	209	298	390	539	565	631

New Zealand

Bruce			45	53	61	72
Wright						22
Total			45	53	61	94
Grand Total	224	328	469	628	667	775

The figure shows that Malaysia is a small market for the company with comparatively modest growth. Australia is a big market of some long standing that is developing strongly and New Zealand is a relatively new market where it is hoped to add a second buyer in the coming year. This sort of information is useful to management in the context of the narrative of the representative's report and company objectives and enables management to formulate plans and allocate resources accordingly.

In a medium-sized to large company there can be, say, anything from 40 to 100 such visit reports to analyse and co-ordinate. Management's first task is to establish whether or not the aggregated forecasts agree with their own growth objectives. It is unlikely that they will coincide exactly but if they are within, say, five per cent either way, with a little fine tuning this may be acceptable. This five per cent is, of course, the variance on the growth target and not total sales.

A Strategy for International Marketing

The second task of management is to examine the resources available to support such growth. The resources will be production capacity, personnel, information and finance.

Production capacity

Where the company makes only one product, the examination is relatively simple: can we make 108 more units of product? If the answer is yes, the decision will depend upon the examination of other resources but if the answer is no, in the short term, the growth targets must be trimmed to fit the production capacity and, in the medium to long term, consideration must be given to increasing production capacity.

Personnel

It is important for management to look at the work load of existing personnel and to judge if the persons concerned can cope with the projected increase. Representatives, who generally thrive on more business, will welcome the chance to do more business because they will benefit financially pro-rata to their performance. Back-up staff, such as sales administration, may be expected to handle increasing work loads for the same salary with the promise of a lucrative bonus based upon profits. It is vital that management recognizes that a person or group of people in that type of situation can accomplish just so much in a working day and an overload can result in mistakes being made, due to pressure or fatigue, which can be costly for the company. Sacking a person because of failure to achieve management's perception of what ought to be possible generally means that you have lost a good worker and are in a crisis situation. The employment of one or two additional people could have prevented this crisis and usually the company can afford to do this.

Information

Many companies regard the gathering of information as a low-key resource unless it can be obtained at virtually no cost, but this is not practical. If it is going to be useful, it is going to cost money. It is right to question the cost but it is wrong to question the need. We should not proceed without valuable information and we should be prepared to pay for it. Looking at representatives' reports of visits, the information may be regarded as free, especially if they have secured some sales that have more than paid for the trip. So, why do so many companies reject the concept of conducting market research when they are doing it on a regular basis?

Finance

This is a matter of making money available to ensure that advancement can be achieved. The money may be there or it may not, but if the bottom line is that profits can be made if there is further investment, someone has to say yes or no. If the money is not there, do we want to raise it to finance the project?

The result of analysing a number of representatives' reports, coupled with information obtained from other sources and looking at available resources, is that management has to establish a medium and longer term strategy, looking at next year, the next two years, the next five years and even further ahead. It is better that management directs the salesforce drive rather than relying upon the salesforce drive to motivate management. If a company is seriously committed to exporting, it must not simply sit back when sales are going well but must analyse the reasons for success just as diligently as it considers the reasons for failure to achieve targets. Sometimes a good result is due to a situation where a representative has capitalized upon a good opportunity which may never recur, or, if it does, the recurrence is unpredictable.

Experience of business in most fields relies upon the representative's skill but also upon the requirements of the market. It is easy to boast that you can do anything that the buyer wants but, in practice, it may not be possible.

Questions for Discussion

1 ABC Products Ltd manufactures and markets educational games and toys. The business started in 1965 in the United Kingdom but over the intervening years sales to Europe have increased steadily and now the accompanying literature and on-product instructions are produced in English, French,

German and Spanish. The company is now considering further expansion into either Saudi Arabia or Morocco and have sought the assistance of your marketing consultancy.

Advise your client as to how it should evaluate these prospective new markets in order to choose which to enter.

2 After two years of exporting part of their product range to Belgium and Holland, CBC Electronics Ltd now wish to expand their activities as follows:

(a) selling more of their product range into the same markets;

(b) exporting to new markets.

As Export Marketing Director, what factors would you consider in order to undertake these tasks?

3 Antique Sticks Ltd have been manufacturing and marketing reproduction furniture for the past three years and are now interested in entering the export market. They have approached your company, Specialist Export Consultants Ltd, to seek your professional advice on selling to markets outside the United Kingdom. How would you advise them to proceed with the selection and assessment of export markets?

4

Why Is Market Research Needed?

There are many reasons why market research is conducted but broadly these can be summarized as follows:

1 market investment planning;
2 development of products to fit different markets;
3 choosing the appropriate marketing mix; and
4 forecasting.

Let us consider these four activity areas in turn.

Market and Investment Planning

This is treated in depth in later chapters but here we are examining the activity in the context of justifying market research time and expenditure. Generally a company will want to know where it is now and where it wants to be in one, two, five, even ten years. The company has to try to test the commercial viability of these ambitions and initially it will be looking at checking out the feasibility of short-term and medium-term goals. The longer-term objectives will only become a real possibility if the earlier targets are achieved.

If we assume that a company has an established business in one or more markets and if we also assume that the company has enjoyed a degree of success thus far, it is logical to expect the company to want to build upon its past performance in order to optimize its talents and the use of its existing and potential resources. It is not possible to determine current performance but in retrospect we can all see what we did wrong and what we did right, but by then it may be too late to change the overall future outcome.

Before we can launch plans to expand our business we have to examine not only the reasons why we failed to meet certain targets but also why we succeeded in achieving others. Selling products is rarely conducted on a level playing field and, on a particular day, one deal could have set us up for a good result or clobbered us out of sight. It is important to be able to analyse the circumstances surrounding each significant deal and to ascertain whether it was marketing skill or the lack of it that enabled us to secure or lose a contract or whether pure chance determined our fate. Many companies will have invested heavily on the expectation of being able to repeat what turned out to be a fluke, and many others will have withdrawn from a scene where they had lost in similar circumstances.

The rational analysis is vital. Generally, as a sales representative, you will know when you are surprised at gaining business but the euphoria at so doing may conceal the fact that it was a one-off. Most deals are one-off simply because two deals, even to the same buyer, are rarely exactly the same. Regular buyers are, of course, what representatives like most and there are many buyers, particularly of industrial products who, once they feel comfortable with a supplier, are reluctant to change unless that supplier's performance declines significantly. Representatives must be aware of their performance level so that they can predict, with reasonable accuracy, repeat purchase cycles.

Representatives will report the market scene as they see it and may be able to give their company a fair idea of the size of the market, the principal competitors and the company's place in the scheme of things – its market share. If the representative cannot do this, the company should check the total scenario by subscribing to published statistics or buying in the result of omnibus research from market research organizations. Professional market research companies are continuously seeking information either specifically through commissioned work or generally as a background to a particular trade or industry. This latter is termed omnibus research and will normally include the volume and value of products traded and recent trends.

Development of Products to Fit Different Markets

The development of products to fit the requirements of new and existing markets is rather a chicken and egg situation – which comes first? Basically buyers always have a latent interest in products that are new, more efficient, save them money, or give them an edge and sellers are always trying to be one jump ahead of the competition. The dynamics of product development and market expansion are reliant upon these two attitudes. The result is usually a highly competitive and innovative market situation.

Development of products does not always mean improving the product but sometimes trying to make an existing product suitable for, and acceptable to, a new buyer or a new market. Any plans for product development must be linked to a perceived demand from a buyer or market and the commercial viability of such development must always be considered.

Levels of demand for a product, or a specific variation of it, are very important in commercial terms. A small buyer who has specific requirements for 10 units of a product every three months will usually command less attention than a buyer with a demand for 150 units of product per month. The profit margins in respect of the small buyer may be attractive, percentage-wise but profit-wise, the big buyer must win.

Most representatives have a plan that involves trying to sell to new buyers and making repeat sales to existing buyers. Both are important because they represent elements of a sales forecast or, at least, they should. The sale to a new buyer is less likely than the sale to an existing buyer but the latter is not guaranteed. In most cases, except perhaps where the buyer is quite small, buyers will have more than one regular supplier and a number of suppliers trying to make their first sales. We shall examine the mechanics of sales forecasting later in this chapter.

Choosing the Appropriate Marketing Mix

The concept of the marketing mix, which was first devised and developed in the United States of America, is a good example of the analysis and intellectualization of a business activity. Sales of products rarely just happen. They come generally as a result of a synchronization of a number of related activities. It is a common practice, particularly for lecturers teaching students, to explain this by using the mnemonic PPPP (the four Ps), Product, Price, Promotion and Place. Other considerations exist, such as after sales service and seasonality; thinking about the topic in terms of your own business, you would certainly be able to think of several more, but these are the main aspects of the marketing mix so let us consider how market research can assist us in these areas.

In most markets, for most products, price sensitivity exists, which basically means that, all factors being equal, the best price secures the contract. The only real exception to this is in a minority market for an exotic product where it is important for the buyer to pay, and demonstrate that he has paid, a high price and, often, a higher price than others in his peer group, for a particular item. This type of approach can often be found in consumer or consumer durable fields such as fur coats, television or music systems, holidays, cars or houses, but there are many instances in the corporate sector such as computer systems, sponsorship or customer hospitality. A great deal of this extra expenditure is a waste of money in hindsight and is probably also likely to be perceived as such before the event by corporate sceptics, but it happens and will continue to happen.

The majority of exporters, however, gear up their marketing efforts to produce the best price and are, frequently, prepared to revise it downwards in order to secure business.

The ability of a seller to achieve a level of sales at the desired price relies upon the contributions from all elements of the marketing mix. The weight of each contribution ought to be determined from the results of market research.

If we look at the features of the product we are basically looking at the reasons why customers buy or do not buy a product. The concept of value for money will be perceived differently by various buyers according to their needs, their opinions, the influence of others or other factors.

Taking a random scatter across a range of different types of products the features considered most significant in influencing a purchasing decision would include the following.

1 Design – is the product visually or aesthetically pleasing?
2 Ranges of colours and sizes.
3 Functionality – does it work properly and reliably?
4 Ease of use.
5 Availability of spare or replacement parts.
6 Safety factors for such products as children's toys.
7 Taste and smell.
8 Quality of performance.
9 Durability.

You can almost certainly think of many more and these should all be considered when formulating research questionnaires dealing with the reasons why customers buy a particular product. Promotion is an interesting area because it involves spending money on advertising, public relations, special offers and other promotions in anticipation of achieving an improvement in sales. If promotion is to stand a chance of being cost-effective, the company must be fairly confident that its approach will be accepted by both existing and potential buyers. Most of us who watch television, for example, may have favourite advertisements for products because they are amusing, clever or topical but how much do they influence what we buy? We may want a washing powder that gets clothes really clean or a car that is economical to run but do we really believe the claims of the advertisers? Obviously, because we need to have clean clothes and an efficient car, we will choose one of those products on offer but it is important for the manufacturer to know why products are chosen or not chosen and, in the case of consumer products, whether this allegiance will be continued.

If you conduct a survey and the results are different to what you expected, you must adjust your thinking, your emphasis and your marketing mix to meet what customers really want. It does not matter how you perceive the demand and the reasons for it; if the results of your research suggest differently, you must adapt or you will fail.

Coming back to features of the product, these should be the basis of your advertising and promotion. You may want to say that your washing powder gets clothes really clean. As a marketing person, you must ignore the fact that a washing powder should do that and issue your boast because your competitors will surely do so.

There are circumstances where stating the obvious is not applicable or acceptable, such as in the marketing of industrial products. Buyers will not swallow the claim that your product will do what it is supposed to do. If you want to secure their business, you must offer a guarantee of product quality, timely delivery, performance of contract and anything else they might want. There are also products which are saleable because they are unique, special or tailormade such as antiques, jewellery and customized items. In these circumstances, the products must be what they are claimed to be and few sellers would risk the resultant law-suit if they were not.

Forecasting

Market research also contributes significantly to a sales forecast; in fact, this is probably the most important contribution made by market research to export marketing. A sales forecast should be made on the basis that the company can handle it and that it aims to make a profit. In exceptional circumstances, such as the launch of a new product or an attempt to enter a new market, a sales forecast showing a loss may be acceptable but this can only be in the short-term. In any other situation a sales forecast showing a loss must be rejected by management and then they must take the decision as to whether or not to continue the sale of a particular product to a particular market or whether or not they are prepared to inject more resources to make it viable.

Sales forecasts must necessarily incorporate sales expense forecasts and these will be based upon several considerations, such as:

1 past sales and the prospect of repeat sales;
2 potential new sales where there are real prospects of business;
3 potential sales because demand exists in the market, taking an overview;
4 possible or potential lost accounts due to poor performance by the company, competition or the financial problems of existing buyers.

Figure 4.1: Target sales and break-even analysis

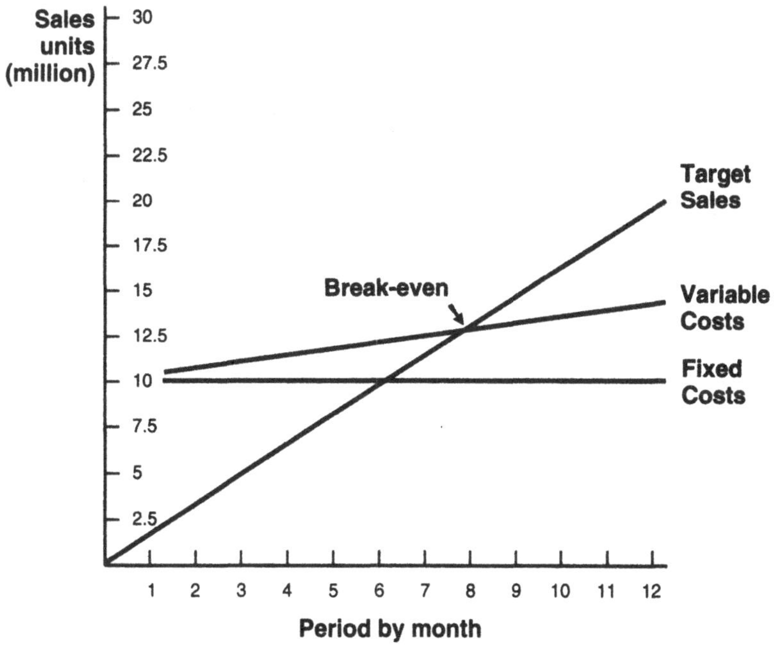

It is important that sales forecasts of individual representatives are combined so that the overall total sales can be related to the company's target and its ability to perform. When this has been done the individual and total targets should be translated into a break-even chart (see figure 4.1) which shows projected sales revenue against fixed and variable costs. Fixed costs will include the overall costs that will be incurred regardless of the sales made such as production, administration and general overheads. The variable costs will be related to actual sales and will cover distribution costs and representatives' commissions where applicable.

In figure 4.1 the sales reflect a target profit where the actual level of sales exceed the combined total of fixed and variable costs. Because the target sales forecast rarely coincide with an over or under performance by the sales force, the final results will vary from the target. If the performance is properly monitored, adjustments can be made so that the target can be reasonably achieved. Looking at figures 4.1, 4.2 and 4.3 we can see the projected target, an over-achievement in the first quarter and an under-achievement in the same period. It is important to pick up significant variances in the early stages of a plan so that corrective measures can be introduced.

Figure 4.2: Sales exceeding target in first quarter and maintained on level basis

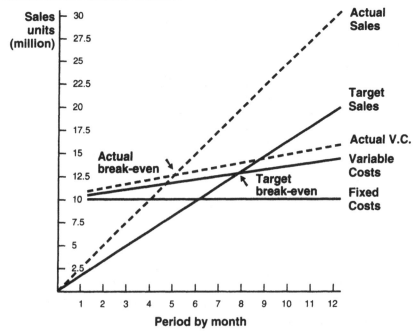

Over-achievement is just as important to detect as under-achievement because to oversell a product can mean that your company is facing claims for late delivery. Underselling against target is serious only for your company in terms of the bottom line, which you may be able to survive, but overselling, particularly in a rising market, can wipe you out. It is important to realize that exporting can mean exports of goods manufactured in your country but can also involve deals done by international trading houses. In the latter case you must be sure that you can cover the goods before you sell short or you will be in deep trouble, but this is presumably a calculated risk which must be watched carefully. No company wants to incur a trading loss but there are times when you may misjudge a market. You must face reality and limit your loss.

Figure 4.3: Corrected sales target due to under-performance in first quarter

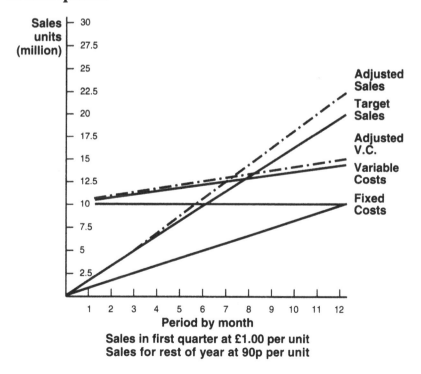

Events will occur during the currency of a forecast which were not envisaged by the representative at the time the forecast was compiled. The most obvious one is that of a buyer going out of business. Although you may be, and should be, covered by insurance, the profit on any goods traded but not shipped or delivered will not be available, nor will the profit on any future business that had been forecasted. The correct procedure in this situation is to adjust the sales forecast to take out any such projected business. It is never pleasant to down-grade your sales figures but it is sensible that you recognize that these sales and profits will not be made.

Questions for Discussion

1 Explain how the findings of market research can make a significant contribution to:
   (a) choosing the appropriate marketing mix, and
   (b) sales forecasting.
2 The sales forecast is essential to effective business planning. Explain how, as Export Marketing Director, you would use a sales forecast as the basis for your future planning, bearing in mind the need for a control facility and a contingency fund.

5

Sources of Information

Information gathered by various means has already been considered in some detail and the use of such information has been demonstrated to be a valuable resource in the export marketing planning process.

Although there are many different sources of export market data, these can be broadly grouped under three headings:

1 internal records;
2 desk research into external sources of published and, sometimes unpublished, information; and
3 field research.

Internal Records

The important aspects of internal records are that they are maintained regularly and systematically, that they should be analysed, or be capable of analysis, into the various areas that will be useful for future management planning and that they are readily accessible to those who need to use them, which should mean every department within the company, although some departments may use more categories than others.

Storage and retrieval of such data through a computerized system is the obvious method but many companies find that their computer cannot yield the required analyses of information that they need because it has not been programmed to do so and, in some cases, does not have the capability to be programmed in this way without considerable additional expense.

Where a company is moving into computerized records or where it is changing, or contemplating changing, its computer system, the decision as to what sort of system is required may be left to senior management who may not appreciate that certain aspects need to be incorporated because they are not personally involved, on a day to day basis, with these activities, or in the regular input of data. It is extremely important that they do appreciate that these aspects exist and that they should be considered when they are making their decisions.

The situation is often difficult because, if the company is moving into computerization for the first time, many members of the company will be unfamiliar with the differences between manual and computerized systems and, in particular, how they must adjust their thinking to take account of a computer's capabilities. They therefore may not be capable of making a useful contribution. If a company is contemplating buying a new computer system, most company members, if they understand the mechanics of the existing system, tend to expect that the new computer system will provide broadly the same service but at an improved level of efficiency and, possibly, with a wider range of available services and programmes.

Computer technology is, however, advancing to such an extent year on year that the mechanics of data input, analysis and retrieval will, for a company that is replacing its existing system with a new one after, say, ten years, be different in many, if not all, respects. It is wise for a company purchasing a computer system to incorporate into the contract an undertaking by the supplier to monitor the operation of the system from its installation until the time it is running smoothly with all bugs removed. This monitoring will include identifying bugs in the programmes requested, the correction of which will be the responsibility of the suppliers at their expense, and enhancements or additional requirements, identified as a result of using the system, for which the company will usually have to pay.

After these caveats, let us assume that you are enjoying a smooth-running, bug-free computer system and that you can input, analyse and retrieve any information that you require. Here are some of the areas of questioning that you will want to direct at your computer system.

1 Sales:
   (a) total business by units and value;
   (b) comparison with last year, last two years and earlier years;
   (c) sales by market, comparison with last year;
   (d) sales by product within a market, comparison with last year;
   (e) sales by customer within market, comparison with last year;
   (f) profit by product, market and customer and comparison with last year.
2 Distribution:
   (a) on-costs of transport, clearance and delivery as well as last year's costs;
   (b) insurance costs and claims record as well as last year's results.
3 Promotion, advertising and public relations:
   (a) amount spent on promotion, advertising and public relations, for current and previous year;
   (b) sponsorship costs for current and previous year;
   (c) changes in levels of sales when advertising or promotion costs increased or decreased.
4 Miscellaneous:
   (a) reports of market visits including analysis of new or increased sales derived from them;
   (b) details of problems, their costs and solutions analysed by buyer and product and whether they are one-off or recurrent;
   (c) payment record of buyers analysed by frequency of late payment.

The list will probably include other topics of interest according to the nature of your business.

The planning of future prospects must be based upon past performance as reflected in your internal records, growth trends over recent years analysed by product and market and your own sales over the period, the degree of market dominance that you have achieved as evidenced by your market share and growth in market share. Internal records must form the basis of any export marketing plan but setting your own performance against the total demand for your products in the various markets is also vital to your plans, and these kinds of data can be obtained only from sources external to your company.

External Desk Research

There are so many external sources of information that can be useful to your company in improving your export performance that it is near impossible to list them all and, even if you could, many of them would not yield anything significantly useful in the context of your own business. In addition, most research into external sources of information will cost you money, so you must know what you are looking for and why, if you are to justify that expense. In some cases, external information may be provided free of charge if the source has a vested interest in providing certain information in the hope that, if you use the information to advantage, they will benefit.

The most obvious of these sources is your bank. Most international banks produce and have available to customers, information about export opportunities. These will range from good, detailed analyses of various markets to rather vaguer suggestions about how you can enter export markets.

Other sources will include Chambers of Commerce, export clubs and government statistics. There are also the omnibus surveys carried out by market research organizations which will give you an overview of your total market at least in some areas.

How much of this external information you will use depends upon how much money you are prepared to spend. The cost-effectiveness of market research has always been a contentious issue because it is always impossible to guarantee that market research will yield positive and profitable results. If it is properly conducted, what it can do is to point out the advantages and disadvantages of a particular course of action. The usefulness of data obtained from external research will only be determined by future events.

Field Research

Where your company has a specific requirement for information about a particular product or market, you must decide whether you want to use your own staff or an outside agency to investigate the scene. Very often, where your sales representatives are dealing directly with an end-user, the salesforce can handle the research project. Field research is original work designed and executed for the use of your company. It is discrete, individual and in most cases unique, although your competitors may be conducting or commissioning similar studies.

Buying in external information which has already been gathered involves a fairly modest expense, say a few hundred pounds Sterling a year, particularly if you take advantage of some of the free services offered by banks and other organizations.

If you are conducting your own field research using the salesforce on routine calls to customers, you cannot ignore the fact that extra costs, above those of the normal visit, will be incurred. The representative may have to allocate an extra hour to each call, resulting in more time spent on the overall visit, which could mean another night's stay in a hotel. In addition, even though the representative will present a report which contains not only the normal routine visit details but also answers to the questions in the specific brief, these will have to be extracted from the overall report and subjected to analysis if they are to be useful to the company. This activity may be entrusted to a member of staff who is suitably qualified in such matters or, if no such person is available within your company, you may give the report to a market research company, together with the appropriate back-up information and ask the company to analyse the data and present a report on its findings.

The first alternative should be properly costed so that your company recognizes the additional work and expense that has been incurred, albeit notionally. The second alternative involves real, rather than notional, expenditure and the difference between the two alternatives may be a notional expenditure of, say, £500 and an actual expense of, say, £1,500. A saving of £1,000 is always important, or should be, but not if you are sacrificing professional analysis and reporting for something that is clearly of poor quality.

In industrial marketing, using the salesforce to carry out market research is often, but not always, satisfactory while in consumer goods or consumer durables, market research by the salesforce alone will rarely be as valuable to your company because there will be more customers, faster repeat-purchase cycles and usually, more competition, and situations are prone to change more quickly than in industrial marketing.

Many companies still resist the commissioning of market research because they cannot justify the costs of the exercise against the benefits that will be derived. The argument for paying the professionals to carry out market studies is that, if the researchers have been properly briefed, the results will be beneficial to the company in either a positive or a negative manner. Positive because profitable opportunities are indicated so that these can be exploited, and negative because serious problems and/or pitfalls are projected and can therefore be avoided. Most companies are seeking to achieve profits but they are also intent upon avoiding losses.

It is important, however, that your company finds out what is happening in the total market and establishes the company's place in that market. This information is crucial to the formulation of marketing planning and, therefore, field research should be undertaken. Your company ought to know who the main operators are and where it stands in the hierarchy of competition.

Let us assume that the total demand in a market territory is 10 million units of product and that there are seven suppliers of the product, three indigenous to the territory and four, including your company, from outside. Let us also assume that the average year on year growth has been two per cent for the past five years. You will almost certainly be able to identify your six competitors and may even know the ranking order in terms of units supplied. What you will need to discover are the buying patterns of the customers and why they choose to buy from certain suppliers and not from others. You may not know all the buyers but there are many business directories available which include names, addresses, and telephone and fax numbers of buyers in many parts of the world, classified under type of business. They may not include every single buyer of a particular product in all of the market territories but they will probably include the large and medium sized companies which could account for 90 per cent of the demand in that territory.

Supposing that you find that there are fifteen buyers in a particular market where your company is operating, four of whom are existing customers and another seven you know but to whom you have made no sales. It should be possible for you to devise a questionnaire to be used by representatives on visits to the territory to elicit information about total volume purchased, frequency of purchase, average size of order and possibly the identity of their existing suppliers. You also need to know the terms on which they buy so that your quotations can be measured fairly by the buyer against the quotations of your competitors.

If you are confident that you can handle this kind of field research, that is fine provided that the research brief to the salesforce is properly co-ordinated. If you do not have that confidence because, say, your involvement in that territory is small and relatively recent, you can use a professional market research company who will generally do a good job if they too have been properly briefed. More about the market research brief later.

Questions for Discussion

1 Explain the contributions that may be made to the formulation of a sales forecast by:
   (a) Desk Research;
   (b) Field Research.
2 To what extent do you consider that a company can conduct its own market research and what value would you attach to market research carried out by a specialist agency?
3 Explain how the findings of market research can make a

significant contribution to:

(a) choosing the appropriate marketing mix;

(b) sales forecasting.

4 Sources of information are vital to export marketing planning and the range of data available has never been wider.

In the context of export market development, how would you assess the value of the following sources?

(a) International fax directories.

(b) Credit reference companies.

6

Methods of Collecting Information

There are many ways in which commercial information can be collected, some of which are more widely used than others. Much will depend upon the type of research your company is contemplating as to which methods will be employed and it is very important that you select the method or methods that will yield the desired information about your existing and/or target markets.

The methods can best be categorized as:

1 Consulting records of past performance, otherwise known as desk research.
2 Communicating with people by face-to-face interviews, mail, fax or telephone.
3 Observing how people behave.
4 Conducting market trials and monitoring the results.

Desk Research

Desk Research can be conducted in the office, examining and analysing the past results of your company in terms of sales, profits, distribution channels, advertising and promotion, payment performance and problem solving. It can also be carried out by writing to, by letter or fax, or visiting, the various organizations where generally relevant information is available and extracts may be obtained. Numerous sources exist such as banks, shipping companies, insurance brokers, road and rail carriers, storage warehouses, credit insurance companies, credit reference companies, the media, Chambers of Commerce, export clubs and government statistics. In some countries these sources are all available while in others the sources of information are more restricted.

Before embarking upon a programme of desk research into external sources of information, it is sensible to establish how much you are prepared to spend on obtaining this information. Before you commit yourself to any expenditure, you should check out the cost of obtaining the information that you require and measure this total cost against your budget. Generally, because companies are reluctant to invest much money in activities that may yield uncertain benefits and because the research team are keen to explore every likely source, the budget will be found to be woefully inadequate. A partial solution to this problem is to seek out free information sources but only if you feel that they can be genuinely useful and not just because they are free, otherwise you are simply wasting your time.

Ultimately, the decision to pay for the desired, and, in the opinion of the research team, the required, information must rest with the decision makers, namely top management and, if you meet resistance to your proposals, you must have sound arguments as to why the company should proceed with the implementation of your ideas.

In the real world, the main consideration in business is the bottom line. Can you, as a sales representative or trader, guarantee that buying this information will result in extra profits? You cannot give such a guarantee so you will always face a situation where your proposals are, basically, indefensible and may not be implemented.

Interviews

The interview between supplier and buyer is a sensitive situation. Both parties are likely to be cagey, but if you pitch your questions in such a way that the buyer finds them interesting and your accompanying remarks flattering, you will usually obtain a good response.

Interviews can be conducted on a face-to-face basis or by telephone. The latter method is often used in connection with advertising research. A consumer may respond to an advertisement in the press or on television and while expecting a response by mail, will sometimes receive a telephone call from the advertiser. Because the consumer's expectations are different form what actually happens, he or she will be defensive and you may lose a potential sale if you push too hard. Many consumers cannot recognize that the telephone is a distancing medium and will feel threatened if you apply pressure. Market research is not the same as marketing and if you behave as though it is, generally you will fail in your attempts to obtain information.

Market research interviews are about finding out what people want and may be the prelude to sales, but they should not be used as a sales pitch, because many of your interviewees will withdraw and you may never get them back.

Even in industrial marketing, materials buyers will have experienced hard selling and cheap prices which have not resulted in satisfactory performance and they will therefore be sceptical of potential new suppliers using the same approach. If you are trying to sell to industry, take the trouble to visit the potential buyer, present your credentials and let the buyer see your face. Then you may obtain valuable information. Patience is often an anathema to a marketing person but it is necessary to establish a sound relationship with a potential buyer if you are to gain his or her confidence and trust.

Research by mail or fax is more impersonal than either the face-to-face or the telephone interview and should always be followed up by a telephone call and, if the response is encouraging, maybe a visit. It is an obvious statement but a letter or fax seeking information should be carefully phrased and presented. It is best to open with a succinct summary of your company's business, stressing the positive areas such as number of years in the trade, volume of business and markets where you operate, provided that these are impressive. Next you must clearly state the information that you are seeking and make it clear that this is a fact-finding exercise which you may or may not seek to develop further, depending upon what information you obtain. Be positive in your approach but avoid appearing patronising.

Response rates to mail or fax communications, even when followed by a telephone call, are generally poor as they are with any type of mailshot. The follow-up telephone call can help to improve the response rate or at least give you a good idea of how many useful responses you are likely to receive.

A significant factor here is your ability to identify the target respondent. With consumer and consumer durable mail surveys, you are generally working from lists of names and addresses, most of whom will not be interested in responding unless you offer an incentive, such as a free gift, and that can prove expensive. In the case of an industrial survey, where you may be able to consult fax directories that are analysed by type of business, you will have a better chance of securing responses because the recipients of your fax are actually buyers of the product that you are selling.

Observation

Observation is an interesting dimension of market research because it encompasses not merely what is happening but also gives the observer the opportunity to analyse the scene. There are many situations where a researcher can observe to advantage. The use of closed circuit television in supermarkets and other large shops and stores is primarily aimed at detecting theft so that security staff can be alerted to intercept the thief before he or she leaves the premises. Equally, it can be used to monitor the success or otherwise of an in-store promotion by recording how many customers stop to consider the promotion and how many of these actually select the promoted item.

Observation can also be carried out to analyse the significance of product positioning within a store. For example, if a supermarket wants to promote the sales of its house brands, it will stack them on shelves that are easily visible to the customer, such as between waist and eye level, with other brands stacked higher or lower than these parameters. Only the most assiduous shoppers who are seeking another brand will explore the shelves at foot or head level.

While it is important for researchers to record as many observations as possible, they must not inhibit customers to the extent that their behaviour changes, because in the context of market research, buyer behaviour is of the utmost significance. People who are conducting face-to-face interviews or hosting consumer panels should also record their observations, especially in respect of attitudinal questions as these will be particularly useful to the editors who are attempting to categorize the answers to open-ended questions.

Test Marketing

Test marketing is an activity used in connection with fast-moving consumer goods (fmcg) and occasionally with consumer durables. The essence of a test market is that it should be a microcosm of the total market and represent as closely as possible the customer profile of the total market. The features of this profile will include sex, age group, income group, size of family, buying influence and so on. The mix of features will vary according to the nature of the product. By consulting research of demographic analyses you can then select areas within one or more regions that most closely match the total market profile. Consideration must be given to promotion facilities and distribution arrangements with the market territory and the various divisions thereof.

In the United Kingdom, certain criteria are used to select a test market area and readers who are indigenous to that area or familiar with it will recognize the criteria. For those readers who are not familiar with the UK scene, they may still be able to identify common, or equivalent, aspects in their own countries. If you cannot fairly closely match the features of your national consumer profile to one or more of the regions, you may be wise to avoid using the test market as a research medium but in the UK and in some other countries, this is a common practice. For example, in England, certain cities and towns have become favourite targets for companies contemplating test marketing because their demographic profiles conform very closely with the national profile. Examples are Newcastle and Southampton; if a company selects one of these cities there is a very good chance of customer reaction in that area reflecting the probable national reaction.

Generally, test marketing is used as a pre-test for the launch of a new product, although sometimes it is used to assess the appeal and demand for a new version of an existing product. Classically the procedure for conducting a test market operation is as follows. Your company draws up a plan for the launch of the new or improved product on a a national scale with target sales for, say the first year, identifying also the target expenditure on promotion and distribution. The company should then look at the percentage of the national market that the test market represents and, if the test market exercise is to last for three months, target sales for the test market over this period will be 25 per cent of the test market's annual share, subject to adjustment for any seasonal variations.

For example, if your company is targeting sales of 500,000 units of product in the first year and your target market, in terms of demographic considerations, is two per cent of the total market, your expectation from the test market operation will be two per cent of 500,000 units divided by four, which is 2,500 units of product. Generally speaking, if your company gets within 80 per cent of the target, it will proceed with the national launch.

The golden rule with test marketing is that if the test market does not meet your minimum criteria, you should not proceed with the national launch. This does not necessarily mean an abandonment of your plans but you may decide to introduce variations in the product specifications, promotion and distribution and try another test.

It is important to remember that since you are targeting in your first three month test market sales of 2,500 units of product against a first year national target of 500,000, you must also scale down your promotion and distribution budgets in the same proportion. This will sometimes present a problem because there will always be minimum costs in these areas and these may be higher than your budget. If your company achieves its test market target of sales within the predetermined tolerance, you should not be too concerned that you have spent more in the areas of promotion and distribution than is strictly correct because firstly, it is necessary to do so to get the job done, and secondly, when you come to the national launch, you will be able to take advantage of economies of scale. For example, if you run a television advertisement six times in three months, you may not attract any discounts whereas if you run the advertisements nationally networked over a one year period you will attract discounts for continuity, or series as it is known, which may more than offset your overspending in the test market stage.

Questions and Questionnaires

The questionnaire, and the questions that it comprises, will be examined in more depth in later chapters, but you should remember that, even where you are not using a questionnaire for interviewer or respondent completion, you should still work out what questions you want answered before you commence your research. The construction and phrasing of the questions is vital to all methods of collecting information. The important criteria in deciding these factors are what you want to find out and why you want the information.

Constructing a questionnaire is one of the more difficult tasks in market research, not because it is difficult to ask questions but because you want the answers to be useful to your company. In addition you will want the respondents to react to your questions with understanding of why you are asking them. If you can achieve this, you will obtain the quality of information that you require. It is crucial that you are able to persuade the respondents that their answers are significant and that you consider their responses to be important. If you can conduct your survey in this tenor you have a better chance of obtaining useful information.

Sampling Techniques

Choosing who to question out of a population of several million people must rely upon a representative sample of the population. With fast moving consumer goods, you will generally have no real idea of the consumer profile so you are obliged to use random sampling. This method relies upon the theory that any randomly selected sample will be representative of the whole market and this is a reasonably accurate assessment if your product type is likely to be purchased by most people, or family groups.

Once you have made your random sample selection from an appropriate sampling frame such as, in the United Kingdom, the Electoral Register or the Postcode Address File, you will be able to devise certain questions that will enable you to build up respondent profiles. This is done by the use of classification questions which seek information about the respondent, such as name, address, sex, age group, occupation, income group, hobbies and so on.

If you can identify specific characteristics of customers, whether they be personal or corporate details, you may decide to draw your sample based on a quota basis. In the case of private consumers, this will be based upon income group, size of family, region of residence, sex, age group and so on, while for company analysis you will be looking at size of turnover, number of employees and number of units purchased.

You must always allow in your questioning for areas where you are uncertain about all the possible answers and request respondents to indicate their own alternatives. No company is omniscient and should never believe that it is.

Questions for Discussion

1 Write short notes on the following:
   (a) test marketing;
   (b) face-to-face interviews;
   (c) postal questionnaires.
2 Test marketing and observational techniques play a significant part in the provision of market research data. Explain how each technique is carried out, giving examples.

7

The Market Research Brief

The market research brief is a document that clearly sets out the objectives of the survey, the tasks to be performed and the universe to be surveyed and it will incorporate a time scale for the research programme and an affordable budget (usually with a reserve for unpredictable contingencies).

Using In-House Staff

The brief will take broadly the same form, whether the company is proposing to use its own staff to conduct the survey or employ the services of a specialist market research organization. The own staff method has the advantages that the personnel involved will be aware of company objectives and be familiar with the specific products and markets and it will involve less expense as the company may be able to incorporate the research into their normal activities. The disadvantages could include a possible lack of objectivity in their approach to the task and unfamiliarity with current market research practices.

Using a Market Research Agency

Compared with using your own staff to carry out the research, the use of market research agencies will be relatively more expensive, but professionally more skilled and experienced. Although agency staff will be less familiar with specific products and markets and may not detect obvious anomalies in the research findings, they will probably be more objective in their approach and in their treatment of data.

The market research brief is created against a background that encompasses the worlds of the pushy, fired-up sales representative and the calm, considered and probably relatively pedestrian researcher who is basically a seeker of truth. Some ground rules, therefore, have to be set if the two are to gel and accept each other's work as compatible.

The following guidelines have proved to be useful for many companies and market research organizations. Some difficulties will always arise because there will be a problem of reconciling the activities of marketing with those of market research, because they require a different approach, but here are the suggested guidelines, bearing in mind that the marketing objectives are paramount.

1 The brief must be interpreted in the same way by both parties. This may mean that, due to the stated differences in expertise and the approach to a situation, a compromise on interpretation may have to be reached in order that an appropriate brief is achieved.

2 The brief must not require irrelevant data to be obtained. Obviously it is very tempting for your company to require, while the respondent is being interviewed, that he or she should be asked as many questions as possible, although your company must be able to justify to itself why each question needs to be asked.

3 The brief must correctly identify the universes to be sampled and questioned, which in this context means the total market. It is essential to have a clear profile of customers in the market place. These will probably include not only your existing buyers but also those that you are trying to secure as future customers. It is possible to argue that, on the basis of time and expense, the research should be concentrated on improving sales to existing customers in order to enhance market share, but the marketing man will never pass up the

chance to sell to a new buyer, so the research should be comprehensive.

4 The brief should also determine the measurement of the right variables. This generally involves the use of behavioural questions such as:

(a) Have you ever bought Brand X?

(b) What quantity do you buy per week/month?

(c) Where do you buy Brand X?

(d) Why do you buy Product X?

Not only should the right variables be included in the survey but they should be evaluated with the best degree of accuracy available.

Supposing the research brief is concerned with conducting media advertising research, your company is more likely to be concerned with group, for example, family, ratings than with individual ratings of the advertisements, especially if the products being promoted are fast moving consumer goods. The impact of an advertisement, say on television, may depend upon the frequency of its repetition and the nature of its approach such as humour, cleverness or topicality.

Timing of interviews may be critical in the context of how well the respondent remembers the advertisement. Obviously, if the campaign is fairly intensive and the slant of the material is subtle or funny or if the advertisement is the latest in a series with a common theme, with some viewers the advertisements will have developed almost as a cult and respondents will react enthusiastically when questioned about them, often when they do not actually buy the product.

Various forms of research methods can be used, such as simultaneous interviews, either while the advertisement is being screened, or shortly afterwards, one-day aided recall, usually by a house call, street interviews showing the respondent a still shot of the advertisement, or seven-day aided recall which would be similar to the one-day aided recall where the interview might be conducted in the street or at the point of sale.

Another form of advertising research is the use of customer panels. These are generally organized in one of two ways. The panellists are invited to attend a kind of seminar where they are asked to contribute answers to a number of general and specific questions about their buying habits and their feelings about various products. An alternative is for a company to build up a consumer panel of users of their product from whom the company will receive regular feedback either by mail, personal interviews or preferably a combination of the two, about price, performance, availability, ease of use and so on, of various products. These panels, by whatever means they are operated, must be compiled in such a way that they constitute a proper representative sample of the customer profile.

Preparing the Brief

A market research brief can be written to cover any aspect, or aspects, of commercial activity. The most important criteria for writing the brief are objectives, methods, timescale and cost. These are all fairly straightforward concepts. Your company's objectives should be clear – you know what you want to achieve. As regards method, you may have your own ideas as to how the research is to be accomplished but, if you are commissioning the research, you should listen to professional advice. Your deadlines are likely to be vital so the timescale will be of the utmost importance. What you can afford or are prepared to spend is a matter for your company to decide. In the last analysis, the decision is yours.

The market research brief is usually devised from the contributions of a number of persons and/or departments. If your company has decided to commission the research from outside your own resources, once you have set the parameters of the research, you should arrange a meeting with the market research company. It is a good idea to send them an outline of what you require with timescale and budget so that they can come to the first meeting with some relevant proposals.

It is likely that the fist meeting will be exploratory, with the market research company trying to present acceptable proposals without having an intimate knowledge of your business, and your company being somewhat cautious because, maybe, you have not worked with this organization before. It is really necessary for both parties to take a positive attitude. Your company is committed to nothing unless it wants to be and the market research organization would like to do a good job as it could lead to future business. At this first meeting, however, your company, as the client, must establish that you can work satisfactorily with the market research company and you must emerge from that first meeting satisfied that both parties have the same understanding of what is required.

Compromises will probably be reached concerning budget and timescale and you must be happy that you can live with these compromises. You may even have to yield to the suggestion that your concept of the methods used to obtain the required information can be improved but you cannot, and must not, deviate from your objectives in commissioning the survey.

There will usually be a second meeting to confirm that both parties are in broad agreement with the revised details of the commissioned work and several more to monitor the progress of the project.

It is probably wise, if your company is unfamiliar with the commissioning of market research or if you have not used a particular company in the past, to ask several agencies to quote for the business. Even if your company is well-experienced in this field, it is probably advisable that you shop around. Many companies feel comfortable with what they know and avoid considering new alternatives. It costs nothing to ask and your company may find an alternative that shows you have been paying too much or getting fairly poor service in the past.

If your company decides to use its own staff to conduct the survey, the scene does not really change except that your own staff will know your business. You must ask yourself, and give an honest answer, whether you want your research to be conducted in terms of an objective or subjective approach. If your own staff conduct the survey they will tend to be subjective because they know your business, whereas an outside agency will tend to be objective because they have no real understanding of your business.

The final outcome may not be very different whichever research team you use, although you will have no way of knowing this. There are two schools of thought about the preparation of the brief. One is that the brief should be drawn up by a management team and then discussed and developed at the meetings between the management team and the research team. The other is that management should present the broad principles of the brief to the research team and the brief will then be moulded by discussion between the two parties into the finished article. There is probably nothing to choose between the two methods; the most important factor is that you should not approach the situation cold. If you have some proposals to consider, a dialogue can take place from the outset; if you do not have such proposals, much time will be wasted in attempts to set criteria and parameters.

Taking the various elements of the brief in turn, the setting of objectives is the prerogative of your company's management; they are responsible and accountable for the progress and development of the company's affairs. Precise definitions and interpretation of the objectives may be required of the research team to obtain the desired information and, whereas an own staff research team may challenge certain aspects of the stated objectives, a market research company should not. The budget available and the timescale for the research to be carried out and the results analysed, may determine the research method to be used.

You can start from the premise that you would prefer to have the survey conducted as face-to-face interviews by questionnaire, but if a market research company tells you that the cost of interviewing each respondent is £5 and that the optimum sample size for this research project is 5,000 respondents, the cost of £25,000 may exceed your budget and may be more than you want to pay.

It is unwise to try to reduce the optimum sample size as this may disturb the accuracy factor and thus reduce the level of confidence in the results of the survey. Management, therefore, has two choices: either to increase the budget to the required level or to abandon the research project. There is not really any middle ground.

You can insist that the sample size be reduced to, say, 4,000, the cost of which fits into your budget, but you are taking a chance which may work out for you or it may not. There is no guarantee that the recommended optimum sample will be more successful than one of a different size, but most market research companies are basing their recommendations on past experience and they know that their reputations are on the line if they are wrong. It is probably advisable to take the recommendations of the professionals in this matter.

The method of drawing a sample ought to be straightforward. As has been previously stated, if you have a clear and acceptable profile of your customer you can safely opt for a quota sample where the selection of respondents is based on known characteristics. Where you do not have this perception, you may be obliged to use a random sampling method to select your respondents.

The first approach is concerned with filling quota slots and where you fall short or overshoot the quotas you can adjust the results statistically. In the case of random sampling, you do not know in advance anything about the people or companies that you will interview but you can find out about them during the interviews and thus obtain information to enable you to categorize them by various characteristics. This will enable you to use the quota sampling method in any further surveys if you wish.

Drawing a quota sample is purely mathematical and fairly easy to do. First, you must find out the national characteristics of the adult population by sex, age group, income group and so on. If you are intending to employ a market research company to carry out the survey, they will have access to these statistics but if you are planning to use your own staff to conduct the research, you can obtain them from any advertising agency, preferably one that you use as they will probably provide the information at no cost. If you do not employ an advertising agency, any medium that you use to advertise your products will generally be happy to give you free access to these statistics. If you do not advertise, you can usually buy extracts of government demographic statistics.

Secondly, you must decide which of the various categories you propose to use to construct your quota sample. In the case of consumer and consumer durable goods, the usual practice is to select any three from sex, age group, income group, region of residence, occupation of head of household or chief earner, size of family and so on. If you are conducting an industrial

survey, you will probably want to cover all significant characteristics such as annual turnover, analysed by a range of values –
number of employees, for example small (say, up to 25), medium
(26-150), large (151 plus), location, including number of branches,
range of products and so on.

Thirdly, once you have selected your characteristics for the
quota sample you must prepare a quota grid. This will tell you
precisely how many interviews you must conduct with persons
or companies that have all of the characteristics that you have
chosen. If you are looking at a sample size of 5,000 where the
chosen characteristics are sex, age group and income group you
will analyse the respondents in terms of national demographic
statistics. An example of this is shown in figure 7.1.

Figure 7.1: Constructing a quota sample grid

Sample size: 5000 adult respondents
Characteristics used:
   Age Group: 18-30: 25%;   31-45: 30%;   46-60: 25%;
                Over 60: 20%
   Sex: Male: 45%; Female: 55%
   Region: North: 20%; South: 25%; East: 40%; West: 15%

Sex within Region (Age group)		18-30	31-45	46-60	Over 60	Totals
North	Male	112.5	135	112.5	90	450
	Female	137.5	165	137.5	110	550
South	Male	140.6	168.7	140.6	112.5	562.4
	Female	171.8	206.2	171.8	137.5	687.3
East	Male	225	270	225	180	900
	Female	275	330	275	220	1100
West	Male	84.4	101.3	84.4	67.5	337.6
	Female	103.2	123.8	103.2	82.5	412.7
Totals		1250	1500	1250	1000	5000

Note: Where quotas are not whole numbers, round up or down

to whole numbers. The company's editor will weight the responses back to the true percentage.

You must remember that it is rarely possible to ensure that interviewers fill their quota correctly because:

1 They are seeking to interview people who meet all of the criteria.
2 They are working with time restraints.

Most interviewers in a quota sample situation do not meet their targets for these reasons, and therefore a statistical adjustment must be made. This is called weighting a sample.

What happens is that the number of interviews analysed by target characteristics is compared with the actual characteristics of the respondents interviewed and an adjustment is made, in an attempt to arrive at an accurate analysis of customer attitude and behaviour towards the product in terms of the nature of the buyer. An example of this analysis is given in a later chapter.

A final few words about the structure of the budget is relevant here to ensure that all aspects of the project have been covered. The various elements will include the following.

1 The cost of carrying out the survey which will comprise:
   (a) the preparatory work which will include the design and printing of the questionnaire, the construction of the sample and the allocation of the work load to the research team; and
   (b) the conducting of the survey.
2 The analysis of the findings.
3 Editing and categorizing the answers to non pre-coded questions.
4 Producing the survey report.
5 A contingency fund to cover unforeseen events, for example delays in one or more of the above activities which may threaten the target finish date so that more resources have to be allocated to counteract the effect of the delays.

If you are planning to conduct 5,000 interviews over a period

of, say, one month and the budget for this including preparation, analysis, editing and production of the report is £25,000,
anything between 10 and 20 per cent should be added as a
reserve against contingencies. Where you have under-estimated
the contingency fund you will have to expend more resources
or risk the failure of the survey. Where you have overestimated
this requirement, this will add to the bottom line, that is, become
an extra profit.

Questions for Discussion

1 Explain the difference between random sampling and quota
sampling and state, with examples, how and when you would
use each method.
2 Upon what criteria would you construct your budget for conducting a market research survey and how would you justify
the expenditure in terms of cost-benefit analysis.

8

Questions and Questionnaires

Whether you are conducting a formal interview or desk research into external sources of information or analysing your own internal records, you will have to draw up a list of questions to which you need answers. You also need to know why you are asking these questions and how you propose to use the information that you obtain. It is sensible to imagine in all cases that you are conducting an interview and to try to remain objective. Your reasons for enquiring into various areas of commercial activity will, necessarily, be subjective because these reasons will relate to the objectives of your company, but the manner in which you seek to obtain information must be objective if you are to avoid looking at only the beneficial aspects and ignoring the problematical, or potentially problematical aspects. It is all too easy for a company to view information in the context of its own objectives but it is essential to recognize that these must be considered against the broad spectrum of the total market.

Your own plans for expansion and development are very important to you, and that is as it should be but, in the market place your competitors will have similar ambitions and may be, even as you are making your plans, making their own. The patterns of product marketing have only so many permutations and some of your competitors may be thinking along the same lines as you. It is, therefore, essential that you have the best information upon which to base your plans and this is why the framing of questions and the constructions of questions is so important.

The questionnaire is probably the most significant element in the whole market research activity. As a formalized document, it is used in interviews of consumers and industrialists, in postal and telephone surveys, in desk research and even in observation situations.

The key factors in any market research plan are:

1 What do we need to know?
2 Who can give us this information?
3 How can we obtain the information we need?
4 What will we do with this information?

All of these are important questions. The first will reflect the objectives of the company, the second will feature the target respondents, the third will require the selection of the appropriate research method and the fourth will be concerned with our use of the information.

It is important that your company knows the answers to these questions otherwise the resultant data will be of less use to you than you had predicted.

The Objectives of the Survey

As a result of these various areas of questioning you will decide upon your general and specific objectives. General objectives state the overall requirements of the marketing plan which could include:

1 Overall target sales in all products to all markets.
2 Entry into new markets.
3 Increase of overall market share.

Specific objectives relate to objectives in respect of products or markets and will therefore include:

1 Target sales to new markets.
2 Target sales of new products.

3 Increase of sales to existing markets.

The research will normally be designed to obtain both quantitative and qualitative data. In consumer surveys the main emphasis will be upon quantitative aspects because of the value of being able to produce reliable statistical analyses of customer profiles and buyer behaviour. Qualitative data is also used to obtain opinions and attitudes of customers, for instance towards your company's advertising and promotions.

In industrial surveys where there will be relatively few buyers of a specific product, component or raw material in a particular market territory, while it is still important to collect quantitative or hard data, obtaining qualitative or soft data will assume a higher profile. This is because you will be able to use this information to refine your product so that contract performance and after sales service can meet the precise individual needs of your customers.

The following are examples of questions seeking to obtain hard data.

1 What size of product do you usually buy?
   (a) large size (state weight, volume, length as appropriate)
   (b) medium size (weight, volume, length)
   (c) small size (weight, volume, length)
2 How frequently do you buy Product A?
   (a) weekly
   (b) monthly
   (c) every three months
   (d) other (please specify)
3 Where do you normally buy Product A?
   (a) supermarket
   (b) department store
   (c) small local shop
   (d) mobile shop
   (e) other (please specify)

The following are examples of questions seeking to obtain soft data.

1 What is your opinion of Product A?
2 How do you think we could improve Product A?
3 What do you think of the television advertisement for Product A?

The Target Respondent

The identification of the target respondent will involve the analysis of the various characteristics of the customer profile. For buyers of consumer or consumer durable products you will be looking at a combination of some of the following.

1 Age group. How does your product appeal to the young, the middle-aged, the more mature and the elderly?
2 Sex. Are women or men more likely to buy or have the buying influence over the purchase of your product?
3 Size of family. For how many people is the buyer and/or buying influence intending to purchase your product?
4 Income group. Into what category of income do your customers fit, for example up to £10,000, £15,000, £20,000 per annum, or more?
5 Region of residence. Where do your customers live: London, and South East, Midlands, South West, North, or wherever.

If you are marketing industrial products, the characteristics will include:

1 the size of the company;
2 quantity of your product bought; and
3 where the business is located.

Types of Questions

There are types of questions and forms of questions. Types of questions are seeking information about the characteristics of the respondent's behaviour and attitudes. Forms of questions refer to the way in which we construct the question in order to obtain this information.

Types of questions fall into three categories, namely classification, behavioural and attitudinal. Classification questions are used to extrapolate the answers received from a sample of the universe in terms of the known national or total market characteristics. In other words, we are seeking to quantify the various profiles of our customers in terms of the total demand for the product. Classification questions, like the selection of characteristics for drawing a quota sample, will focus upon several areas such as age group, sex, income group or region of residence to establish a range of customer profiles.

Behavioural questions are seeking to find out how people behave in the market place. What do they buy, where and when and how much and how frequently. Ascertaining the degree of brand loyalty and retention of that loyalty is vital to the seller of fast moving consumer goods such as breakfast cereals, washing powders, TV dinners or beverages so that plans can be formulated with confidence.

Attitudinal questions are aimed at finding out why people buy products, their motivations and opinions. Sometimes these are nebulous in terms of statistical analysis but they are valuable just the same because they reflect the approach of individuals to your product and those of others.

Forms of Question

There are three forms of question – dichotomous, multiple-choice and open-ended. Dichotomous comes from the Greek and basically means dividing the answers into two diametrically opposed parts such as yes or no. It is common practice in market research, however, to add a third dimension to catch the undecided, such as 'don't know' or 'can't remember'. It may seem to be a waste of time to have category that comprises indecisiveness or ignorance but it is useful to be able to see the percentage of positive and negative responses in terms of the total number of respondents surveyed. It is a bit like the floating voters in the run-up to a General Election. Sometimes, where the main political parties are evenly matched, it is important to know the percentage of the undecided which may be significant in the final analysis. Some will vote one way, some will vote another way and some may not vote at all.

A good example of a pure dichotomous question is where there are only two options such as in the classification question, sex of the respondent, where the answer will be either male or female. In the modern world, and probably in the past, it is well understood that some males will sometimes behave as though they are females and vice versa, but this scenario is not usually the province of the market researcher.

Multiple-choice questions generally form the core of the market research questionnaire because they allow the research to gather statistical information about known variables. In classification questions, these will include age groups, income groups, region of residence and nature of occupation. In behavioural questions the use is prolific and will cover where goods are purchased, when they are purchased, how often they are purchased, and which brands, sizes and colours are purchased. In attitudinal questions such questions are rarely used unless the researcher is confident that he is aware of the whole gamut of opinion which normally is not possible.

Open-ended questions are seeking personal opinions and attitudes which the researcher generally does not wish to predict or prejudge. In face-to-face interviews the researcher will be asked to record verbatim the words of the respondent which is normally lengthy and may or may not be useful. In self-completion questionnaires the answers will range from the garrulous to the silent and, bearing in mind the fact that the vast majority of mail questionnaires are not returned and, of those that are returned, some are unusable, this type of survey is unlikely to produce much valuable data from open-ended questions.

The types of questions used and the forms they take must fit into a sequence that is both logical and easy to follow by the respondent and, where applicable, the interviewer. The best way in which to achieve this logicality of sequence is to arrange questions in topic groups. The topics should be based upon the general objectives of the survey and the specific objectives relating to each general objective.

For example, if the general objective is to assess your market share, the specific objectives could be to find out which brand the respondent buys, how many units of product are purchased over a stated period and where they buy the product. You could also ask why they prefer the stated brand. If it is your brand you will know what you are doing right for these respondents and, if it is not your brand, you know what you have to do to increase sales.

The sequence in respect of this set of questions will be:

1 Do you buy breakfast cereal? (Dichotomous question.)
2 Which brand do you buy? (Multiple-choice question.)
3 How many packets do you buy per month? (Multiple-choice.)
4 Where do you buy your breakfast cereal? (Multiple-choice.)
5 Why do you prefer this brand? (Multiple-choice or open-ended question.)

If you use a multiple-choice question you suggest various reasons such as price, taste, availability or children's choice and offer an open category where respondents can state other reasons. If you use an open-ended question, it will be left to the editorial team to interpret the answers.

Pre-coding Questions

It is advisable to pre-code all dichotomous and multiple-choice questions to facilitate the analysis of the answers. If these questions are not pre-coded they must be coded after the survey has been conducted. Pre-coding should be used where you are confident that you are aware of the main alternatives and post-survey coding where you are not.

With classification questions, some categories such as age group, sex and income group can be pre-coded with some degree of confidence but others such as hobbies, holidays or type of job may not.

Multiple-choice questions lend themselves to pre-coding provided that you have a fair grasp of buyer behaviour in respect of your product. If you include a free-answer category, this can be dealt with by the editors and all other answers are ready for statistical analysis.

Open-ended questions are rarely pre-coded because the object of the questions is to allow individual answers and these can take many forms and cover a variety of aspects of the question asked.

Figures 8.1 and 8.2 show examples of pre-coded questions.

Figure 8.1: Pre-coding of classification questions

SEX	ANSWER	CODE
MALE		1/X
FEMALE		1/Y

AGE GROUP	ANSWER	CODE
18-25		2/U
26-35		2/V
36-45		2/W
46-55		2/X
56-65		2/Y
OVER 65		2/Z

REGION	ANSWER	CODE
NORTH		3/W
SOUTH		3/X
EAST		3/Y
WEST		3/Z

Pre-coding facilitates the post-research analysis and should be used whenever the vast majority of the answers can be predicted. The codes used are generally from the end of the alphabet to avoid confusion with part questions that include letters from the beginning of the alphabet such as (a), (b) and (c).

The demographic statistics such as sex, age group, income group, region of residence and so on are normally clear-cut but

Figure 8.2: Pre-coding of multiple-choice questions

BRAND CHOICE

BRAND	ANSWER	CODE
CUSTOS		14/T
GIGOU		14/U
PARMA		14/V
MAZEM		14/W
ORCHID		14/X
OTHER		14/Y
NAME		14/Z1

COLOUR PREFERRED

COLOUR	ANSWER	CODE
RED		14/T
BLUE		14/U
GREEN		14/V
YELLOW		14/W
BLACK		14/X
WHITE		14/Y
OTHER		14/Z

WHERE PURCHASED

SHOP	ANSWER	CODE
SUPERMARKET		18/V
CORNER SHOP		18/W
DEPART. STORE		18/X
MOBILE SHOP		18/Y
OTHER		18/Z
PLEASE SPECIFY		

with behavioural characteristics there will always be exceptions to your perceived patterns of behaviour. Although these are generally likely to be minority groups, you should always include an extra category of answer for two reasons:

1 because you may have misread your market profile and these contributions are important; and
2 some of the responses may open up new opportunities for you to exploit.

Looking at figures 8.1 and 8.2 we can see two contrasting forms. In the case of classification questions your respondents are of a certain sex, age group and region of residence, while in the case of behavioural questions, you probably know most of the answer categories but acknowledge that there may be some that you do not know.

While you as a professional or student, or otherwise interested party, may understand the basic concepts of market analysis and its usefulness to the promotion of business, most customers do not, although many industrial buyers have a fair grasp of the situation.

If expensive market research is not to be wasted you must ensure that you ask the right questions. The specimen questionnaire depicted in figure 8.3 attempts to do this but you must remember that in any market research survey, we are trying to hit the right spots in terms of what we want to do.

Figure 8.3: Specimen questionnaire

Let us assume that we are conducting a market research survey into the consumer profile, buying habits and attitude towards one of our products, Vita-Orange, a health drink.

General Objectives

(a) To establish the customer profile of Vita-Orange.
(b) To find out customer behaviour and attitude to the product.
(c) To explore the potential for expansion of sales.

Specific Objectives

To discover:

(a) Demographic characteristics of customers.
(b) Customer buying habits.
(c) Brand preference.
(d) Reasons for brand preference.

Questionnaire

1 Sex of respondent
Male
Female

2 Age group of respondent
16-25
26-35
36-45
46-55
56-65
65 or over

3 Income group of respondent/family
Up to £10,000
£10,001-£15,000
£15,001-£20,000
£20,001-£25,000
£25,001-£30,000
Over £30,000

4 Region of residence of respondent
London and South East
South of England
Wales and West of
England
Midlands
North East
North West
Scotland
Northern Ireland

5 Size of family unit
(a)
Single person
Two persons
Three persons
Four persons
Five persons
Six or more persons

(b) How many children in
family group

One
Two
Three or more

6 Do you buy orange or other juices?

Yes
No

If the answer is No, thank the respondent
and close the interview.

7 Which flavours do you buy?

Orange
Lemon
Grapefruit
Blackcurrant
Other, please specify

If answer is orange ask question 8.
If not, thank the respondent and close interview.

8 Which brand of orange juice
do you buy?

Tang
L'Orange
Buzz
Vita-Orange
Other please specify

9 How many 1 litre cartons do you
normally buy per week?

One
Two
Three
More than three

10 Where do you usually buy your
orange juice?

Supermarket
Local shop
Other, please specify

11 Why do you buy a particular brand
of orange juice?

Taste
Price
Availability
Other please specify

12 Why do you consider it important to include orange juice in your family's diet?

13 Can you remember any advertisement for orange juice that appealed to you?   Yes

                                                     No

If yes,   (a) what brand was being advertised?
             (b) what appealed to you about the advertisement?

Note: (b) You can suggest reasons for the appeal in which case it will be a multiple-choice question or not, in which case it will be an open-ended question.

Editing of Answers

This is a specialist field. The editorial team must look at the answers to open-ended questions and decide whether and how they can categorize them. In most cases the respondents are saying the same thing in different words, but sometimes they are not.

How do you deal with this situation? You have to decide whether you want to cater for the needs of small buyers and if you value their business. If you do, you will probably want to get involved with the micro-market which can be very rewarding. The editorial team's job is to establish how significant the minority findings of the research are to the general and specific objectives of the company. If you are intending to extend your business, on whatever scale, they will be; if you are not, forget the micro-scale.

The editors' analysis of the answers to open-ended questions will usually be instinctive and sometimes they will be way out. It is very difficult to translate what people say into what they will do and, if your company relies upon editorial interpretation too precisely, you may be embarrassed by future results. The other concern will be involved with the 'other please specify' options where the respondents are saying that they do not fit into your prescribed pattern but do something different. Here the editorial concept of reality is likely to be much more valuable and usable.

For example, the open answers to a multiple-choice question about brand choice should yield data on buyers of minor brands after the major brands have been specifically listed. Collectively, though, the percentage of buyers of the minor brands may be greater than that of one or more of the major brands. From this conclusion, the editors can look at buying patterns and reasons for purchase of those respondents who nominated these minor brands, and plans can be made to try to win over some of these customers to your brand. This plan will obviously be based upon statistical information because you will be basing your actions upon the findings of a small sample which, however carefully drawn, will still be small.

The editors' findings will be added to the analyses of the hard data obtained and both will be incorporated into the survey report which will be compiled by the research team and submitted to management. It is very important to prepare these reports with great care, stating the research method, the size of sample and sampling technique used, and the dates and time scale of the survey. The report should be carefully filed as it can serve as an excellent starting point for a follow-up survey or a future survey using the same basic parameters.

Questions for Discussion

1 It is vital to the decision-making process that information researched from the market place is relevant to your company's marketing objectives and this is particularly true of commissioned market research. Explain how the answers to the following types of questions can contribute to such decision making.
   (a) Classification questions.
   (b) Behavioural questions.
   (c) Attitudinal questions.
2 (a) What do you understand by the terms 'hard data' and 'soft data'.

(b) How would you expect such data to contribute to performance analysis and future planning.

3 Two of the most important aspects of sound market research are the preparation of the questionnaire and the analysis of the findings. As a consultant with Target Market Research International, how would you explain to your clients the significance of the following activities:

(a) pre-coding questions;

(b) editing of answers.

4 You work for Worldwide Research Ltd as a customer account executive and one of your clients, Exotic Cruises Ltd, has asked you to prepare a questionnaire aimed at existing and potential customers to determine their behaviour and opinions in respect of the company's existing services, and to obtain suggestions as to favoured innovations.

Draw up a draft questionnaire to submit to this client.

9

The Export Marketing Plan

Business planning generally adopts the following rules.

1 Set objectives over a stated time scale. In other words, establish where you are now and where you want to be in one year, two years, five years and ten years' time. It is desirable for a company to be able to plan for positive continuity of its business although, in some economic climates, planning to survive until next week, next month or next year, concentrates the minds of the planners wonderfully.

2 Establish that you have already, or have access to, adequate resources to meet these objectives. Naturally, the predominant resource in most plans is funding, but, if you are a manufacturer, you must have the required production capacity, reliable suppliers of raw materials components and services, as well as the appropriate personnel to cope with the tasks involved.

3 Decide what you have to do in order to implement your plan. This will include research into the viability of your plan and the elements of the marketing mix that must be tailored to fit the requirements of your plan, which will involve both timescale and the correct coincidence of events.

4 Devise a method of monitoring the progress of your plan so that any deviations from the predicted scale of development of the plan can be quickly identified and corrective measures taken. It is often the case that you will discover, through this

monitoring process, that you are falling short of your projected target, but sometimes you will find that you are
exceeding your predictions of sales. Both are equally commercially embarrassing, under-achieving because your company
may be facing a loss-making situation and over-achieving
because you do not have the resources to meet your commitments.

Setting the Objectives

Marketing objectives should reflect how your company wants to
perform over, say, the next 12 months. Some examples of such
objectives are as follows.

1 Increase in overall sales and, where you are selling more
   than one product, individual target sales for each product.
2 Improvement of market share. Unless you are a major player
   on the world scene, you will usually set targets for improvement of market share by individual territory. If you are a major
   player, while the analysis of the various products within market targets is important, your global target for all products in
   all territories may be more important in terms of your world
   status and your ability to dominate and influence buying
   decisions on a grand scale.
3 Introduction of a new product to one or more markets. You
   will have to decide if you are going to use a test marketing
   exercise to launch the product which would be the normal, and
   safe, approach with a new product. The possible exceptions
   might include the launch of a seasonal product such as a
   children's toy or game aimed at the Christmas trade. If you test
   market the product, you give your competitors the chance to
   see your product and launch one of their own to challenge
   your sales prospects. Another example is when you are producing very high-tech equipment and you have a significant
   edge in the market because of a new technique or formula.
   Here you cannot afford to wait or the benefits of your research
   and development programme may not yield the results that
   they merit and you require.

Marketing objectives, as has been said several times in this book, must be related to a timescale. Also, some objectives may be set in the context of the short-term, such as six months, while others may relate to a medium or longer term, such as one year and five years.

Let us examine the case of AEB Ltd, who have been in the export market for three years and are seeking to expand and develop over the next five years. Their overall growth target is 30 per cent over the five year period, with annual growth rates of 4, 5, 6, 7 and 8 per cent measured against the pre-start-year target sales.

These overall targets will comprise a series of individual targets analysed by product within market against timescale. If AEB Ltd are marketing, say, four product groups to five markets at the start of the plan and their objective is to extend these to five products or product groups within six markets over the five year period, each product's market objective must be set with care and consideration of all strengths, weaknesses, opportunities or threats that are present or likely to occur during the five year period. This, of course, is impossible to do at the outset of a five year plan and it is, therefore, useful in this type of situation to use the back up of a rolling forecast which can monitor and adjust the actual performance against the plan; this will be dealt with in more detail in the next chapter.

It is important, however, to remember that some projections are cautious, particularly if the sales representatives or traders do not want to be seen by management to fall short of their forecast sales, and that some are ambitious because the sales force is feeling bullish or management has insisted that cautious forecasts are unacceptable and must be enhanced.

Resources Required to Meet the Objectives

These fall into four main categories:

1 production capacity or the availability of product;
2 finance;

3 personnel; and
4 information.

Most companies like to plan for growth, although in a recession, the ability not to lose ground may realistically be the best you can expect. Your company must be realistic about its future prospects and plans and the sales and marketing budgets, as well as those of production and administration, must be carefully calculated. Selling products and services is always a tough business because of competitive pressures and changes in levels of demand. In some economic climates, such as inflation or recession, the absence of a stable level of demand will make selling conditions quite different. In an inflationary climate costs and prices will rise and larger companies will generally be able to cope with these conditions better than smaller companies because they can take advantage of economies of scale. In a recession many costs will be constant or subject to minimal increases but as competitive pressures build up, sales margins will fall to dangerous and sometimes disastrous levels.

Assuming that your company is already in business making and selling products, you should start planning your next year's activities and resource requirements well in advance of the start date. As an existing business, most of next year's activities will probably be broadly similar to those of this year and you will, therefore, be able to make projections based upon the current year's performance, with the necessary adjustments to cover required changes in levels of production, sales, personnel, costs and other factors.

Your budget to cover your plan will consist of two basic elements – projected income and projected expenditure. Part of your expenditure can be calculated fairly accurately because this will be incurred regardless of how many units of product you sell. These are known as fixed costs and will include rent or lease payments on your factory and offices, wages and salaries, heating and lighting as well as depreciation on machinery and equipment. The other forms of expenditure are known as variable costs and will include production and distribution expenses, commissions paid to agents and sales representatives, advertising and promotion and research and development. Some of these may be variable according to the number of units produced and some, although still variable, may not be strictly in proportion to the number of units produced.

Sales and Profit Targets to Meet Objectives

A useful aid to establishing the structure of the financial plan is the break-even chart which shows the elements of cost and projected sales income against the timescale of the plan.

Let us assume that your company is planning for next year based on a sales forecast of 600,000 units of product at a sales price of £5 per unit. Let us also assume that your fixed costs are £1.2m and your variable costs are £2 per unit. Your projected sales income will be 600,000 x £5 = £3m; your variable costs will be 600,000 x £2 = £1.2m, which when added to fixed costs, also £1.2m, will make total projected cost of £2.4m. Thus your projected profit will be £600,000. See figure 9.1.

Figure 9.1: Break-even analysis

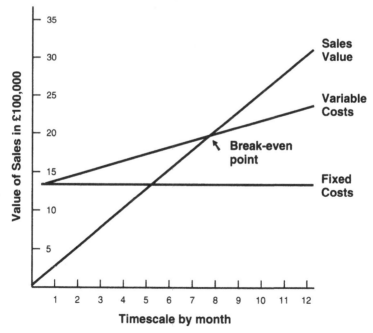

89

From the break-even chart, you can see that at the point where 400,000 units have been sold, with a sales value of £2m, your company will break-even and for the remaining 200,000 units of product sold, you will make a profit of £3 per unit and, if you achieve your target sales, a target profit of £600,000. It is extremely rare for a company to hit its target sales income and target expenditure right on the button. How you try to cope with this situation will be dealt with in the next chapter where we will be monitoring the progress of the plan.

Once you have devised your plan and set your budget you must ensure that everyone concerned is aware of what the targets are and what needs to be done to achieve these targets.

The sales force will certainly be aware of what they are expected to achieve during the period of the plan because they will have made contributions to the target sales forecast. Other departments of the company, such as production, must be made aware of what is required of them and must be advised to report any problems that may cause the pattern of the plan to be disturbed. For example, if you are using imported materials in your production you must be comfortable with the shipment and delivery schedules. You will have forward contracts with your suppliers and you must be able to rely upon them to keep you advised of any problems. If any of them do not do this you must seriously consider replacing them with more reliable suppliers. The longstanding personal relationship will count for nothing if they let you down and you have to stop production. As a manufacturer, you must be able to rely upon your suppliers of raw materials or components to supply as per contract.

Management must keep in regular touch with the sales force, probably upon a weekly basis either by reports of business done or by meetings or, preferably, both. If, as is usual, the sales force is on a bonus or commission scheme, they will want to be performing in accordance with their targets and, if they are not, your management need to know this and the individual sales representatives will need to explain why they are not. Management may not like the reasons for under performance and may decide that the sales representative is inefficient and may seek to replace that person. This is the world of business and sometimes sacking sales staff brings improvement in performance and sometimes it does not. The important aspect of analysing sales performance is to be aware of the prevailing market circumstances. It is essential that management is aware of these circumstances so that they can take measures to mitigate their effect and understand the reasons for variance against target.

Although your export marketing plan may be thought at the outset to be workable, signs may appear at an early stage that matters are not proceeding as expected and some remedial action will be necessary. By the time the new year's plan is under way the performance against target of the previous year's plan will be known and from these results some indications should emerge as to which areas of the new year's plan need adjustment. Management must ensure that all departments immediately report any problems with the implementation of their part of the plan as all departments must operate as a cohesive unit if the plan is to succeed. Regular reporting, say monthly, is vital particularly since the monitoring activity will be taking a retrospective overview of the performance so far. The next chapter deals with monitoring the progress of the plan.

Questions for Discussion

1 After one year of marketing their product to Malaysia where they achieved 90 per cent of target sales and 75 per cent of target profit, Ajax Components Ltd are planning their second year's business to this market. Their objectives are:
   (a) to maintain sales at their present level; and
   (b) to increase profits to the first year pro-rata target.
   Draw up a plan.
2 Outline the salient features of an export marketing plan with particular reference to objectives, resources, implementation and control.

10

Monitoring and Control of the Plan

The success of an export marketing plan depends not only upon the appropriateness of the criteria by which it has been devised, but also upon the overview of the plan as it unfolds. The performance of a plan precisely according to target objectives is virtually impossible to achieve and this situation must be recognized and addressed by the planners. It is necessary, therefore, for the planning team to decide, in advance of the plan's implementation, how they will monitor the performance of the plan and what tolerances they will accept. Because sales forecasting is notoriously difficult and because it is unlikely that your company will be able to predict all of the significant events of the coming year, the monitoring of performance against targets must be conducted against a background of corporate objectives and an understanding of market conditions.

There are various schools of thought about target performance. Some will take the view that, if a sales representative or trader is expected to earn profits of £250,000 in the year, which is about £5,000 a week, this target must be achieved fairly early on or he or she will never catch up. Others will look at the seasonality of demand and will accept that there will be lows and highs. The important thing is that the highs must be fully exploited because, in the low periods, the opportunity will not be there to over-achieve.

Some retailers in many countries consider that about 60 per cent of their business will come in the two-month period prior to Christmas. This will relate not only to trade in traditional Christmas goods such as Christmas cards, trees, puddings, cakes, mince pies and so on, but also in the sale of various items which will be purchased as Christmas presents. If you take this situation to its logical conclusion, many retailers are relying upon Christmas sales not only to make a profit on the year's trading but to break-even.

Periodic Checks on Performance Against Targets

Many companies rely upon a computer printout to tell them what business has been achieved compared with the predicted level of business. This approach has several disadvantages. Take the case of a sales representative of computer systems whose target is to sell £1m worth of product in a year. In 1992 nothing is sold although hard work has secured an order. In 1993, products to the value of £3m are sold and, having under-achieved by 100 per cent in 1992, the representative has over-achieved by 200 per cent in 1993.

It is important to take a sensible view of such matters. Some products sell in great numbers of units, such as baked beans or breakfast cereals, and some sell in relatively few numbers such as computer systems. If you expect a computer system sales representative to sell £1m worth of product per year and £3m worth of product is sold in the second year, you may have considered sacking this person at the end of the first year as nothing was sold during year one. Know your product and know your market if you are going to be able to monitor the performance of a plan efficiently.

If the product is properly forecasted with the seasonal variations, it should be relatively easy to decide when to take remedial action and when these are normal circumstances.

Computer printouts can be useful in monitoring the plan although to do an effective job you may have to consider aspects that are not specifically covered by the plan. For example, one computer printout often called aged debt analysis will tell you which buyers are late with payment for goods. It is very important to watch this carefully for long overdue debts and regular offenders. It may sometimes be necessary to stop deliveries against contracts if the amount overdue becomes significant, say up to £50,000 or more.

It is wise for your company to operate a system of trading and credit limits based upon commercial and financial information obtained from companies such as Dun and Bradstreet and NCM. Working within these limits is not sufficient in itself. You must highlight slow payers and watch their accounts very carefully and, if you are concerned about the position of the account, make some confidential enquiries to see if that customer is in financial difficulties. Business is not worth doing if you do not get paid or if a large chunk of your profit is lost in interest charges. It is better to leave these sorts of buyers to the competition and let them have the problem.

Monitoring the plan involves looking at all aspects necessary for you to meet your commitments. You must be able to identify problems with production, distribution, administration and so on, particularly where there may be a danger of contractual default, as in many trades the consequences can be financially and commercially painful.

The main focus, however, must be upon sales performance against sales targets. If these targets are not met, you will not achieve your target profit.

As has been mentioned earlier in this chapter, regular appraisals are necessary and, if problems are seen to exist, the reasons for them must be identified and remedial action taken. For example, suppose in the situation illustrated in figure 9.1 where level sales were predicted throughout the year, instead of £750,000 worth of sales being achieved within the first quarter, only £650,000 were made. If this trend continued throughout the year, your sales would fall short of target by £400,000, which would seriously damage your bottom line. You decide to reduce the price to £4.50 per unit and an immediate improvement is evident. (See figure 10.1.) By launching a promotion for the rest of the year, you achieve total sales income of £3.25m, yielding a total of £996,665 which has effectively retrieved the situation. Generally, failure to sell is down to price, although quality of performance also plays a part. It is clear that the exporter must organize his resources and monitor his performance.

Figure 10.1: Correcting a shortfall in sales

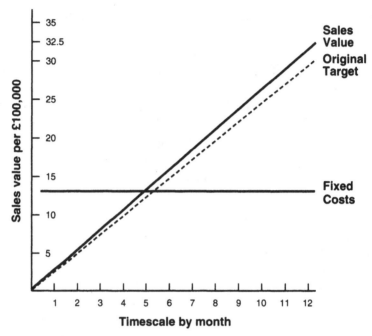

Questions for Discussion

1 What would you do if at the six month monitoring stage:
   (a) Sales were below target?
   (b) Sales were above target?
2 The sales forecast is essential to effective business planning. Explain how, as Export Marketing Director, you would use a sales forecast as the basis for your future planning, bearing in mind the need for a monitoring facility and a contingency plan with funding.

11

Numerical and Statistical Analysis

Presentation of Data by Graph, Chart and Diagram

The presentation of data may take several forms such as graphs, charts and diagrams. Which one you decide to use will depend on what significant features of the data you wish to portray. In the case of a graph, this is excellent for plotting trends and seasonal variations in demand. Take the following example.

Your company in the past year had forecasted total sales as 50,000 units of product and actual performance was 55,000 units of product, or 10 per cent above target. The product is quasi seasonal with forecasts for the four quarters of the year as follows.

First quarter   12,000 units
Second quarter 15,000 units
Third quarter   15,000 units
Fourth quarter   8,000 units

Your performance was:

First quarter   13,500 units
Second quarter 16,700 units
Third quarter   15,300 units
Fourth quarter   9,500 units

Figure 11.1 presents the forecasted and actual sales on the same graph. Further analysis into the reasons for the variance should be conducted and compared with previous years to determine whether any trend or pattern in the shift in seasonality can be established. If it can, future forecasts should reflect this pattern. If it cannot, you will probably continue to make your forecasts on a 'one-off' basis.

Figure 11.1: Sales of product by unit for 1993, forecasted and actual

The use of charts is very appropriate when you wish to illustrate a share of the whole scene. This could be your company's market share or it could be your total sales analysed by market.

Using the second example, let us assume that your export sales for 1993 totalled £10 million and that the breakdown by market was as follows.

Market	Sales in £m	% of total
Belgium	0.95	9.5
Holland	2.0	20.0
Germany	2.5	25.0
Spain	0.5	5.0
Australia	1.5	15.0
United States	2.0	20.0
Brazil	0.55	5.5
Totals	10.00	100.00

This can be illustrated by a pie chart – see figure 11.2.

Figure 11.2: Analysis of export sales by market

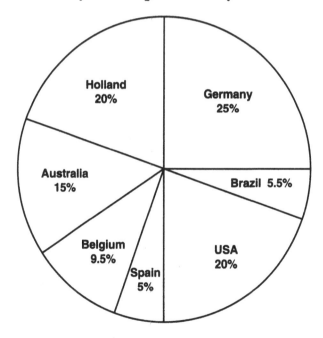

Diagrams can be in a number of forms to illustrate the overall position such as Critical Path Analysis or a particular aspect of your company's activities such as 'Top 10 Buyers'. Look at Figure 11.3 for an example of the latter.

Figure 11.3: Top ten customers 1993

Customer	Units Sold	Profit (000s)	% of Total
Corkell	10K	0.5	1.48
Stevenger	17K	0.9	2.66
Feltham	32K	1.5	4.43
Scully	15K	0.8	2.36
Beaulieu	105K	5.7	16.80
Chattergee	22K	1.1	3.25
Caskey	88K	4.6	13.60
Prufrach	75K	3.9	11.53
Van Klenk	102K	5.0	14.80
Steltenburg	82K	4.5	13.30
Others	75K	5.0	14.80
Total	623K	33.8	100

Analysis of National World Markets

The analysis of national world markets for your products is a very useful exercise as it enables you to establish not only the values and volumes and the location of demand but also variations of these due to seasonality where this is applicable. It also allows you to keep abreast of changing conditions and the opening up of new markets by territory and product and for these reasons the exercise should be repeated regularly, say on an annual basis.

In many countries of the world official statistics exist showing the volume of sales by product or product type with a breakdown into domestically produced and imported goods. Most of the larger market research companies have international connections with many parts of the world and you should be able to purchase this information from them. Once your company has become established in a market territory you can keep up to date through your selling agents or distributors and through market visits.

Calculating Market Share

By conducting market research in a territory you will be able to identify your market share from an analysis of the answers to questions such as:

1 What brand do you buy?
2 How often do you buy this product in a year?
3 Do you ever buy another brand? If yes
  (a) Which other brand do you buy?
  (b) How often do you buy this brand in a year?

Supposing that your company conducted a survey of 5,000 consumers, an analysis of the group of questions given above might yield the results shown in figure 11.4.

Figure 11.4: Purchasers of product by brand based upon sample of 5,000 responses

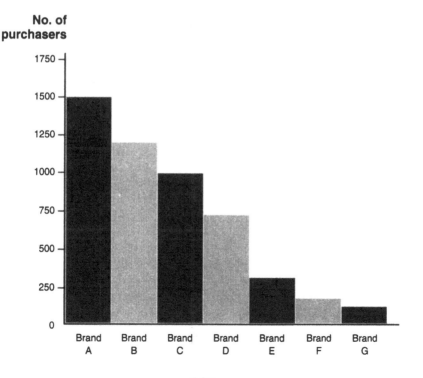

Comparative Performance

Some of the most important aspects of data analysis are covered by questions such as 'what did we aim to do?' and 'what did we do?', 'what did we do this year?' and 'what did we do last year?'

Publicly quoted companies are always under minute scrutiny by the business media and variances in year-on-year results can have a significant effect upon share prices.

Looking at estimates against actuals is a vital task for management and this should be done at least on a quarterly basis so that shortfalls and overshoots can be tackled promptly. It is presumed here that forecasts will take into account any seasonal aspect of product demand so that unnecessary panic measures are not taken.

Figure 11.5 shows that, after a slow start, management injected more resources into promotion of the product with the result that sales improved and the end of year result was less than half a per cent below target.

Figure 11.5: Comparison of estimated sales against actual sales, with corrective action, by units of product

	First Quarter	Second Quarter	Third Quarter	Fourth Quarter	Total Units
Estimate	5,000	7,000	4,000	9,000	25,000
Actual	4,800	6,000	5,600	8,500	24,900
Action	Salesforce Pep-talk	More Promotion	None	N/A	

When forecasting, it is likely that your company will take the previous year's result as a base. Generally, management will be going for growth and will expect to see an improvement in this year's performance over last year's. While the treatment illustrated in figure 11.5 may be applied, the comparative outcome will show that the performance has been more successful or less successful in achieving the desired growth. After Quarter 1 a small shortfall has occurred and management decide to rally the troops. This clearly does not work because at the half-way point, performance is 10 per cent down on target. Management decides that more salesforce support is required and their decision is rewarded as the lost ground is not only recovered but also they are now ahead of the game. As a result, they decide to take no corrective action and the year ends with performance marginally short of target.

Sensible managements will always use comparisons of 'this time' and 'last time' to monitor performance in the current year, also bearing in mind the target for the current year. This will usually be based upon profits rather than unit sales and figure 11.6 gives an example of this in operation.

Figure 11.6: This year/last year comparisons plotted against this year target profits (£000s)

	Target This Year	Performance This Year	Performance Last Year
First Quarter	275	260	250
Second Quarter	325	330	300
Third Quarter	450	480	400
Fourth Quarter	400	420	350
Total	1450	1490	1300

Looking at figure 11.6 we can see that generally the performance against target has been good after a relatively slow start and a final extra £400,000 profits above target has been achieved.

In most cases, in both estimates against actuals and this year/ last year comparisons, management of results will probably be conducted on a monthly, or even a weekly basis, rather than a quarterly basis.

The most important points to note are to know where you are in terms of where you want to be at any time so that you can take any necessary corrective action.

12

Budgets

Much has been written in this book about gathering of information for management planning purposes and together we have looked at sales forecasting and carrying out market research through market visits and a presence at trade exhibitions. The theory of such planning and research, if it is to be accomplished in reality, must be supported by adequate financial resources.

Any business activity such as production, sales, promotion or distribution must be carefully analysed in terms of the financial resources required. In other words, a budget must be calculated and be presented to top management for approval. All activity budgets must be collated and synthesized by top management to ascertain if the individual and collective activities can be accommodated in terms of the available financial resources over the required timescale.

If the aggregated estimate of expense cannot be met by available financial resources, the board of directors, or whatever the status of top management may be, must decide whether to restrict certain areas of spending or to seek to raise additional financial resources. It is always tempting for management, where the former premise obtains, to cut spending in areas that are not obviously profit or earnings related, such as market research and advertising and not to penalize the sharp end of the business, which must always be sales. This is a point of view that can usually be justified but it may be one that is short-term and short-sighted.

Anyone can manage successfully with hindsight but decisions have to be made before actions are taken and the top management of any organization is there to be shot at if they get it wrong.

Budgets, like forecasts, are, and can only be, estimates. For this reason, you should always include an element of cost for possible or unforeseen contingencies. This allows you, in most cases, to adjust your spending to meet particular events or circumstances when they occur without the need for a board meeting to approve the extra expense. In deadline situations, the time to wait for a decision may not be affordable or commercially sensible. If you have got your expense forecast horribly wrong, you are in trouble anyway and it may be prudent to stop everything until management decide how, or if, to proceed.

This chapter deals with budgets in terms of analysing the components of the budget and attempting to challenge and validate the various elements against the information from which they are derived.

Sales Budget

A sales budget will include the following elements.

1 Target sales by value.
2 Cost of target sales, for example manufacturing or purchase cost.
3 Salesforce salaries and commission.
4 Salesforce expenses, for example travel, accommodation, subsistence.
5 Management expenses.

Target sales by value

This is the aggregated sales forecasts of the members of the salesforce that has been accepted by management as reasonable in terms of the company's sales and profit objectives.

Cost of target sales

If you are a manufacturer you will take the figures from the production budget to establish what the goods cost to produce. If you are a merchant house you will tend to use a method of deducting oncosts from the sales value. These oncosts may include freight, insurance, finance, storage costs, delivery costs and credit insurance.

Salesforce salaries

These are known before the budget period begins and, if salary reviews are conducted on an annual basis, these estimates are likely to be fairly firm. Where commission forms a significant part of the sales representative's remuneration, actual sales must be checked at, say, monthly intervals so that the commission may be paid promptly.

Salesforce expenses

Usually sales representatives men will submit travel plans for approval and these are usually accompanied by an estimate of the costs of travel, accommodation and subsistence.

Management expenses

These are usually a notional addition to the overall expenses and are usually based upon the amount of time that management devotes to the sales activity in terms of the salaries of the managers involved. Sometimes, but not often, it is taken as part of management's job and is not costed, but generally it should be.

Figure 12.1 shows an example of a sales budget.

Other Types of Budget

Other types of budget include advertising and promotion, production, distribution and administration. The first of these is intended to examine the correlation between advertising and promotional expenditure and increased sales. The second will indicate your company's ability to be competitive in the market place. The third will echo the second and the fourth will show how well you can retain the profits achieved in the sales budget.

13

Some Other Numerical and Statistical Aspects

Use of Averages

In modern business, management use averages as a tool of monitoring performance against target. Profits are always more important than unit sales but, obviously, if more product is sold, more profit should result. If your company has been located in a recession-beset economy, the anxiety of top management will require weekly analysis of performance against target whereas, in a healthier economic environment, assessments may be made less frequently, say monthly.

Under pressure, however, sales made with profit below target may be criticized by management, but sensibly will be welcomed. The sales representative is always trying to secure business and must be allowed the discretion to book a sale at a lower margin rather than lose the deal to competition.

The averages that will often be used by management are the mean, the median and the mode. Basically the mean is the average of the values under consideration, the median is the middle value of the range and the mode is the most frequently occurring value.

If we look at the sales forecasts and actual performances of the individual members of your salesforce we are able to calculate these averages. See figure 13.1. The results show that the mean for actual against forecasted sales is up by about £10,000, the median is down by £2,500 and the mode is down by £15,000. In the case of the median, this is because three of the top six, BJW, VJP and LAB, performed above the average positive variance against only one, GWH, in the bottom six. In the case of the mode, this is because the bottom two, FRH and GWH, performed comparatively better than the two sales representatives above them, WJS and ORL.

Figure 13.1: Forecasted sales and actual sales by sales representative

Sales Representative	Forecasted £000s	Actual £000s
BJW	510	535
MPD	490	495
JGC	475	485
VJP	450	480
LAB	440	455
JJB	420	410
DGT	400	405
CRD	380	390
WJS	375	385
ORL	375	375
FRH	350	360
GWH	345	360
TOTAL	5010	5135
Mean	417.5	427.916
Median	410	407.5
Mode	375	360

The time series is a useful tool for management because it shows the changing values of a variable over time. This can relate to population, export sales or levels of disposable income. There are various factors that influence a time series such as seasonal variations, the overall trend and unusual movements which do not follow any predictable pattern.

Seasonal variations can be determined by use of moving averages. If you are working on an analysis of sales on a quarterly basis and you look at any four-quarter period, such successive periods will show not only the seasonality but also a trend. Nothing is totally predictable in business so it is very important that blips are identified quickly. Sometimes these are warnings of a change in an established pattern and sometimes they are simply one-offs which may or may not recur. See figure 13.2.

Figure 13.2: Time series analysis of sales over three years

		Moving average of four quarters
Quarterly sales		**Moving average**
£000s		
Quarter 1	230	
Quarter 2	270	
Quarter 3	260	
Quarter 4	270	257.5
Quarter 5	250	262.5
Quarter 6	260	260
Quarter 7	290	267.5
Quarter 8	300	275
Quarter 9	310	290
Quarter 10	310	302.5
Quarter 11	280	300
Quarter 12	300	300

The use of index numbers is a way of comparing relative values over a period of time. In the United Kingdom the Retail Price Index is commonly referred to as a guide to price inflation and other countries have similar indices which reflect trends in their economies.

Other indexes used include share prices on the Stock Exchange, changes in house prices and movements in currency exchange rates. The use of such indices can be both informative and deceptive, depending upon how they are analysed.

In the export field unit sales may have increased year on year but in terms of home currency earnings they may have fallen because of exchange rates variations.

If you are a United Kingdom exporter selling goods to the United States in US dollars where your average profit is five per cent you may find that you are selling more product but making very little more, or even less profit in sterling terms. See figure 13.3.

Figure 13.3: Profits from export sales indexed against year 1 average exchange rate

Year	Sales US $ (000)s	Profit US $ (000)s	Average Exchange Rate	Profit £ (000)s	Index
1	500	25	1.75	14,285	100
2	600	30	1.60	18.750	109.38
3	750	37.5	1.65	22,727	106.6
4	700	35	1.70	20,588	102.94
5	775	38.75	1.75	22,142	100
6	800	40	1.80	22,222	97.22
7	830	41.5	1.85	22,432	94.59
8	900	45	1.80	25,000	97.22
9	850	42.5	1.85	22,973	94.59
10	920	46	1.80	25,555	97.22

In conclusion it is hoped that all readers of this book will have found it helpful in their understanding of International Marketing Research and to those of you who are students, may I offer every good wish for your future careers.

14

Suggested Answers to Questions for Discussion

Chapter 1

Question 1

As Export Marketing Director of CBC Electronics, you have two objectives to address:

1 selling more of their product range to Belgium and Holland; and
2 exporting to new markets.

While these are distinctly separate objectives and require different approaches, there is a link in that you can use your experience of selling to Belgium and Holland as a guide to your being able to sell to new markets.

When selling more of your product range to your existing markets, a key factor may be whether there is a clear link between those products that you already sell and those that you wish to sell. If there is such a link, your existing business should help you to sell these new products, provided that your price competitiveness and your contract performance are consistent with your existing business and you must ensure that they are.

If there is not a clear link between the products that you already sell and those that you wish to sell, you may be looking at business with existing buyers but you may also be considering business to new buyers. In the latter case, you are facing, in many ways, the same situation that you would be facing in sales to a new market, and the same discretion of checking financial status and credit worthiness must be applied.

The exhilaration of obtaining an order from a new customer must be tempered by these considerations if you are to feel comfortable about this new customer. Deals may go wrong later but you must be happy about a sale to a new customer at the time that the contract is made.

Exporting to new markets, in a sense, is back to square one and this is the right approach. Safe options may be available and these would be generally advisable, unless what appears to be a once-in-a-lifetime situation presents itself. It is difficult to advise about how to proceed in such circumstances – you could achieve a resounding result or it could be a nightmare scenario. Generally, you will only know how good or bad it is long after you have signed the contract.

Obviously, expanding into new markets suggests geographically proximate territories, such as Luxembourg, France and Germany or markets that are using the same products. If these two criteria apply, go for that market. You can always target others in the future.

Question 2

A market is a term that is used to describe a territory, a product or a product within a territory. Therefore if you sell only one product, you will have a number of territorial markets for that product. Your global coverage of the market may be five territories so your marketing effort will be directed at five territories. A territory may be a country, a part of a country or several countries, according to how your company designates its selling territories.

Much will depend upon the volume sales of your product but generally it is best to analyse your sales by product within territory and match these against target.

Chapter 2

Question 1

This is a classic, although nice, dilemma to address. Steady growth in European Community markets on the one hand and the interesting potential development on the other.

On a purely profit-earning basis, assuming Burgess Meredith can sustain the six per cent annual growth to the European Community, it would achieve an additional £10m in sales within a little over two years. On a company objectives basis, BM must be looking to expand into other markets or it would not be conducting market research and the Brazilian market survey has yielded very positive results.

There are several courses of action:

(a) Ease down on the European Community growth target to say 3% per annum and make a start in Brazil
(b) Look at ways of increasing production and other activities by raising funding by share issues or borrowing
(c) Do both.

Question 2

(a) Expansion within the European Community is the safer option because of proximity to the existing market and similar marketing and economic conditions.
(b) Eastern Europe is ripe for business development and perhaps a joint-venture or a manufacturing under licence arrangement might be more suitable here.

Chapter 3

Question 1

Morocco is French-speaking and, since the literature and on-product instructions are already available in French, this would seem to indicate Morocco as the obvious choice.

On the other hand, Saudi-Arabia is an extremely wealthy country which has spent vast sums of money on educational projects including the recruitment of teachers of English. This would therefore appear to be a ready-made market for this range of products.

In both markets, however, there would have to be product adaptation particularly in the topics and activities portrayed in the existing products in order to conform to the cultural requirements of the new market.

Question 2

Firstly, you must establish whether or not there is demand for other products in your range by existing markets and if there is demand, whether or not you can sell to the various buyers. If they are existing buyers of your products, the answer is probably in the affirmative but, if you are looking at new buyers, you are looking at a scene similar to that of breaking into a new market.

Secondly, if new buyers are involved, you do at least know the territory, how to get your product to the customer, what are the promotional media available and who are your competitors.

Exporting to new markets requires approximately the same skills and activities that you used when you first began to export your products. The rules will be the same; the circumstances and interpretation of the rules may be different.

As Export Marketing Director, you will want to be seen to be successful but you will probably also want to be seen as innovative and seeking new opportunities. It is probably not a good idea to regard the various objectives of your company as separate options. Sometimes they are complementary to each other and you may benefit by adopting several courses of action.

This question is suggesting that you attempt to do both and you should go for that.

Question 3

Specialist products rarely fit into the general pattern of marketing and sales because it is quite difficult to identify the customer profile. With fast-moving consumer goods, your target market is virtually every household while, with consumer durables such as television sets, video recorders, washing machines, refrigerators, cars and lawn mowers, your products will be of interest to most households most of the time. Industrial raw materials, components, products and services will be in demand by manufacturers, provided that your product and performance and price are acceptable.

Reproduction furniture combines modern technology with classic design and a large part of the developed world has a strong affinity with nostalgia. A British company offering new furniture produced in these classic designs will attract buyers from the United States and any country that has links with the former British Empire and the present British Commonwealth such as Canada, Australia, South Africa and New Zealand.

Chapter 4

Question 1

Market research can make significant contributions to many business activities and the value of these contributions will depend upon why and how the research was conducted. If it is primary research – research that was conducted to ascertain specific information to satisfy specific needs, it will contribute a great deal of valuable information that will help you to formulate your marketing plans. If it is secondary research which may be carried out by a professional market research company, it can still be useful to your planning but it will be as a background of the overall market scene against which to set your planning.

If you ask the right questions, you will get a useful range of answers to enable you to evaluate which features of the marketing mix your customers find important. This exercise is not about proving how right you were in your judgements but more about knowing what your customers want and why they want it.

This knowledge is absolutely vital if you are trying to construct a sales forecast. You may think that you understand your customers perfectly but, if you do not, your sales forecast will fail. The best sales forecast is one that can address the reality of a situation and present the scene as it is.

Question 2

As Export Marketing Director, one of your prime tasks is to co-ordinate the sales forecasts of the members of your export sales team. Forecasts usually fall into two categories, the cautious and the ambitious. Cautious forecasts are usually put forward by those members of the salesforce who feel under threat because of failure to meet their declared targets or are genuinely under pressure to make acceptable levels of sales. Ambitious forecasts are generally propounded by those representatives who think that they know what the management want to hear and they may be buying time.

It is up to you, as Export Marketing Director, to judge the validity of each salesman's forecast so that you can make your plans accordingly. It is best to look at the record of each sales representative and, if there are significant forecasts of different patterns of trade indicated, have one or more discussions with these people before you make your final decision.

Chapter 5

Question 1

Desk research may be conducted into your company's internal records or into published or unpublished data produced outside the company. Obviously your own performance will contribute greatly to the production of a sales forecast but external information will help to put this in the context of the total market.

Field research is conducted mainly to find out answers to questions that will have a specific bearing upon your business. Some of this research will tell you how you rate in the market and this is important to your plans.

Question 2

The conduct of market research may be carried out by your company or by a specialist agency. Which you choose may depend upon the degree of expertise that you consider will exist. Most market research companies have great expertise in researching consumer and consumer durable products while, with industrial products, your own staff can probably do a better job.

Deciding which to use may well depend upon the depth of information required and the timescale within which it is required. On the one hand, you have the professional researcher who probably does not understand your product and, on the other hand, you have the sales representatives who knows the product thoroughly but may not know what questions to ask.

Question 3

Market research involves a number of activities which include looking at recent data and trying to forecast future results.

Planning aspects will include choosing the right marketing mix and sales forecasting.

Basically, choosing the right marketing mix involves looking at what worked in the past and making the necessary adjustments, while making the sales forecast relies upon salesforce prediction of results.

Question 4

Obtaining information is important and if you are aware of what is available you may be able to make better decisions.

International fax directories are a revelation and a revolution. Identify your product and you can find many customers around the world. A simple fax message and you could be in business.

The more serious side of business, and this is usually anathema to most marketing men, is the credit worthiness of customers. As a sales representative, you find someone who wants to buy your product and you are ecstatic, but can they pay? A check with a credit reference agency will usually allay your fears.

Chapter 6

Question 1

(a) Test marketing involves the use of a micro-market exercise to establish whether you have an acceptable product and whether you have presented it in the right way. Test markets are usually identified in terms of customer characteristics and buying patterns. It is usually advisable to set up a test market where you are planning to launch a new consumer product.

(b) Face-to-face questions usually yield the best information, certainly in terms of quality, because the one to one situation allows the interviewer the opportunity to conduct in-depth questioning where appropriate. This is particularly relevant in the case of industrial market research where detailed information about the activities and requirements of individual companies is essential to developing a sound and profitable relationship.

(c) Postal questionnaires have the reputation of yielding the fewest and least useful responses of any research method. Generally this reputation is deserved but the existence of an extensive range of specialist mailing lists in many countries allows the researcher the opportunity of identifying the ideal target respondent with a great deal of accuracy and, where specialist lists are used appropriately, response rates are better. Even so, useful responses will rarely exceed 10 per cent of postal questionnaires dispatched.

Question 2

(a) Test marketing is used to evaluate the soundness of a marketing plan prior to the broadscale launch of a product. The area selected for the test market must be broadly representative of the total market in terms of customer profiles, distribution channels, media and promotional facilities.

(b) Observational techniques are often used in conjunction with other types of research such as face-to-face interviews, in-store promotions and consumer panels, but they can also be free-standing. Most observation research employs the use of recording equipment such as video cameras although personnel will also be used to contribute their interpretations of the activities.

Chapter 7

Question 1

In the context of market research, random sampling is based upon the notion that any person selected for interview is likely to make as valuable a contribution to the research project as any other. One must qualify this idea slightly by saying that the researcher will always be working with a sampling frame such as the electoral register, telephone or fax directories. This means that you will be restricting your universe to those persons who are eligible to vote or those who have a telephone or fax machine and, therefore, by definition, be excluding all other persons. The sampling frame need not be a list; it can be a mathematical device, such as every tenth house in a street.

Generally, however, a random sample is used in connection with the survey of popular activities such as buying washing powder or breakfast cereals since most people do these things and are therefore likely to be able to make a contribution to the research.

Quota samples are drawn in connection with known, or sometimes perceived, characteristics which, in the case of individuals, can be sex, age group, income group or type of job. In many countries, these demographic characteristics are readily available and are used widely by marketing organizations, media advertising analysts, market research and other bodies.

Question 2

A typical market research budget would include the following heads of expenditure:

(a) the preparatory work, such as desk research, design and preparation of the questionnaire, construction of the sampling frame and drawing the sample;
(b) conducting the survey – interviewers' fees and expenses such as postage, telephone calls;
(c) analysis of the findings;
(d) editing the answers to open-ended and other non pre-coded questions;
(e) producing the survey report;
(f) a contingency fund to cover unforeseen events and (or) costs in excess of estimates.

Chapter 8

Question 1

Classification questions are used, as the name suggests, to classify respondents by certain characteristics. In the case of individuals, commonly used classifications relate to sex, age group, income group or region of residence of the respondent. In the case of companies, they will include: nature of business, number of employees, volume and value of business and location of head office. These characteristics help the researcher to identify customer profiles.

Behavioural questions seek to discover the buying patterns and habits of customers such as how much they buy per week, month or year, when they buy and where they buy. In the case of consumer products this enables the sellers to organize their distribution and promotional activities and to combat the advantages enjoyed by the competition.

Attitudinal questions are used to find out what motivates customers to buy a product and their general and specific opinions about, and attitudes towards, the product.

Question 2

(a) Hard data is a term used in market research to define any information that can be statistically analysed. When using a questionnaire as the research method, the answers to all classification and most behavioural questions will yield hard data.

Soft data, by contrast, is information that, in its original form, is incapable of being analysed statistically. Usually soft data is the product of answers to open-ended questions where the editorial team will arrange the answers into broad categories which may then themselves be analysed.

Hard data is the essential basis for performance analysis. You look at your target objectives and you compare these with the results. Any variance must be explained and, here, the use of soft data may make a contribution to such as salesmen's reports.

(b) Planning relies heavily upon performance analysis. The basis of plans will always be past performance even if you are planning not just for growth but also for the elimination of mistakes.

Question 3

(a) Pre-coding questions is a common feature in many question-naires, especially where the sample of respondents is large. Categories of questions that are invariably pre-coded are dichotomous (yes, no, don't know) and multiple-choice where a list of alternatives is given, including a final option to catch all answers not covered by the specific alternatives. The purpose of pre-coding is to facilitate rapid post-survey analysis of the data.

(b) Editing answers is one of the ways in which the hard data base which provides the statistical analysis of the information may be qualified and refined. The editorial team will look at the answers to all questions where the answer categories have not been predetermined and arrange them into groups of answers. The individual group will include answers that have approximately the same meaning in the opinion of the editor.

Question 4

Follow the guidelines in chapter 8 and devise your own questionnaire.

Chapter 9

Question 1

In a real-life situation you will know what quantity of product you have sold and how much profit you have made so the percentages given in this question will have some meaning. To help you to think properly in planning and budgetary terms, it is advisable to put in some values of your own such as last year's target sales were £10m and last year's target profit was £1m. Thus, the actual sales achieved were 90 per cent of target = £9m and the actual profit earned was 75 per cent of target = £750,000.

Looking at the objectives set for the next year, the sales target will be £9m and the target profit will be £900,000. Check out the reasons why you did not achieve target last year. Was it competitive pressure or over-ambitious forecasting? Did you under-estimate costs or were there unexpected problems that caused the shortfall in your profit? Check that your resources are adequate and that your methods of operating the plan are sound but with enough flexibility to allow for smooth adjustments as you proceed.

Question 2

An export marketing plan should involve the following elements.

(a) Objectives. These will be general objectives, such as entering a new market or expanding turnover and specific objectives such as individual product target sales and margins.
(b) Resources. These will generally include:
    (i)   funding,
    (ii)   personnel,
    (iii) communications,
    (iv) production,
    (v)   distribution,
    (vi) management services,

(vii) information.

(c) Method of implementation set against a timescale.

(d) Monitoring and control mechanisms.

(e) The budget for the plan which should include a contingency fund.

Chapter 10

Question 1

(a) If sales at the six month stage were below target, the position will presumably have worsened significantly since the last control check and if this is being exercised on a monthly basis, it is likely that most of the problem has occurred during the past month. Many targets have at least a notional tolerance and it could be that the five previous monthly checks showed performance within target tolerance. The problem that caused the latest month's performance to slip out of the target tolerance range might have been a single incident which might be a freak occurrence which is unlikely to recur. In this case, no action may be necessary except to increase the frequency of monitoring checks to two-weekly intervals to see if the performance returns to acceptable levels. If the shortfall was caused by other circumstances, the necessary corrective action must be taken quickly.

(b) Where sales are above the upper tolerance target at the six month checkpoint the same criteria apply as for the shortfall but you must look at the overall trend during the six month period to see if there has been a steady increase. You may need to consider contingency funding if you are happy for this trend to continue.

Question 2

The sales forecast contributes to future business planning as follows:

it shows the target sales;
it states the fixed and variable costs;
it indicates the target profit;
it enables a break-even analysis to be made;
it shows any seasonality in sales demand;
it gives a timescale.

Index